CONTENTS

RECONNECTING WITH TREES

THE WONDER IS THAT WE CAN SEE THESE TREES AND NOT WONDER MORE.

—Ralph Waldo Emerson, nineteenth-century US writer and poet

For thousands of years, the Mbuti Pygmies made their homes in the rain forest of lands that became the Democratic Republic of the Congo (DRC) in Africa. The villagers who lived nearby feared the darkness and animals in the forest. They cut back the trees to build homes and to farm. But the Mbuti embraced the forest in every aspect of their lives. For food, they hunted forest animals, such as pigs and monkeys. They also gathered forest plants, mushrooms, nuts, fruits, and their favorite food, honey. They made clothing from the leaves and bark of ficus and fig trees. They used long tree limbs and leaves to construct shelters. The forest was also their pharmacy: they made medicine from the oils, bark, and leaves of trees and other plants.

Sunlight filters through the forest in North Cascades National Park in Washington State. Some of the tall trees there are hundreds of years old.

British anthropologist Colin Turnbull studied the Mbuti Pygmies in the 1950s and wrote about their lives in a book called *The Forest People*. A Mbuti man named Moke told Turnbull how his people connected and communicated with the forest:

The forest is a father and a mother to us, and like a father and mother, it gives us everything we need—food, clothing, shelter, warmth . . . and affection. Normally, everything goes

A Mbuti man in the Democratic Republic of the Congo climbs a tree to collect honey. For thousands of years, forest plants and animals have supplied the Mbuti with food, shelter, and clothing.

well because the forest is good to its children, but when things go wrong, there must be a reason. . . . So when something big goes wrong, like illness, bad hunting, or death, it must be because the forest is sleeping and not looking after its children. So what do we do? We wake it up. We wake it up by singing to it, and we do this because we want it to awaken happy. Then everything will be well and good again. So when our world is going well then we also sing to the forest because we want it to share our happiness.

The Mbuti still live in the forests of the northeastern DRC; still obtain food, clothing, and shelter from trees; and still revere their forest homes. They are not the only humans who venerate trees. Trees have been central to human society for thousands of years. Many cultures tell of a "tree of life" from which all other life springs. This concept also appears in twenty-first-century pop culture, including the fantasy/science fiction film *Avatar* (2009). The "tree of souls" in *Avatar* is a giant willowlike tree with a luminescent glow. It connects all living things to one another and to their god, Eywa, on the planet Pandora. The people on Pandora live in large trees. All the planet's trees are connected and communicate with one another.

LIFE-GIVING TREES

Stories of a tree of life or tree of souls are based on the fact that trees are essential for living things. Trees provide shelter, medicine, and food for millions of plant and animal species, including humans. Trees also help cool us. Think about standing under a tree's shade on a hot day. *Ahhhh*.

People have long felt the mental and physical benefits of being around trees, regardless of the temperature. Think about how calming it is to walk in a park or forest compared to walking down a busy city street. Health experts have even found that just looking at a picture of trees can help a person relax.

Water is essential to life on Earth, and trees play a big role in Earth's water cycle. They take up water through their roots and release it into the atmosphere through their leaves. In the process of making food, trees also release oxygen, a gas that humans and other animals must have to live.

DYING FORESTS

Forests are vital to life on Earth, but forests are in trouble. Around the world, humans are cutting down trees to make products such as paper and furniture and to obtain foods such as palm oil. Humans are also clearing forests to build farms, homes, industrial plants, roads, and cities. The loss of forest for any reason is called deforestation.

Forest degradation involves harm to or partial destruction of the forest ecosystem—the community of living and nonliving things in a forest, such as plants, animals, soil, and water, that rely on one another for well-being. Many human activities can degrade forests. For example, when humans pollute the air or water, they might endanger the health of living things in a forest. When humans allow livestock to graze in or near forests, the animals often eat tree seedlings, so they never become adult trees. Forest degradation can be temporary or permanent. Unlike deforestation, the forest still exists, but the trees and other living things there are less healthy than normal and more vulnerable to disease.

For thousands of years, our human ancestors obtained food by hunting animals and gathering wild plants. They cut down a few trees to build tools, boats, or shelters, but they didn't clear large areas of forest. About ten thousand years ago, people in the ancient Middle East began farming. At first, farmers cleared only small areas of land to plant crops. They didn't cut down entire forests. But eventually, human society grew more complex. People cut down large areas of forest to build homes, cities, and large farms. When European settlers migrated to North America in the early seventeenth century, vast forests stretched

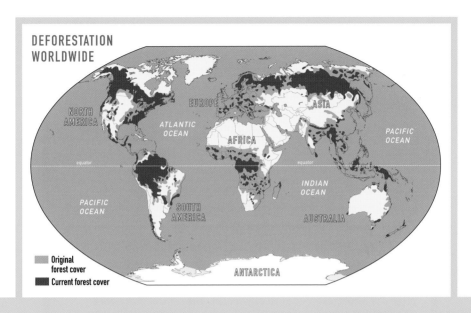

DEFORESTATION WORLDWIDE

NORTH AMERICA
EUROPE
ASIA
ATLANTIC OCEAN
AFRICA
PACIFIC OCEAN
equator
equator
INDIAN OCEAN
PACIFIC OCEAN
SOUTH AMERICA
AUSTRALIA
ANTARCTICA

Original forest cover
Current forest cover

Over thousands of years, humans have destroyed more than half of Earth's forests to build cities and farms.

from the Atlantic Ocean to the Great Plains, with other large forests out west. In lands that would become the United States, forests covered about 1,023 million acres (414 million ha), nearly half the size of the present-day nation. Since the first Europeans arrived, Americans have cut down about 256 million acres (104 million ha) of forest to build farms and cities.

The destruction of forests is happening worldwide. Scientists estimate that in the last eight thousand years, humans have destroyed more than half of Earth's forests. The rate of destruction has increased in modern times. Every year, humans cut down roughly 15.3 billion trees. Between 2000 and 2016, humans deforested areas that, if combined, would be as large as the United States east of the Mississippi River.

Another threat to forests is climate change. By burning fossil fuels (coal, oil, and natural gas) and wood, humans add excess carbon

SCIENTIFIC STUDIES

Scientific studies take several different forms. In an observational study, researchers collect data based on their senses: what they see, hear, touch, and smell. They observe study participants or subjects in their natural state. For example, if biologists want to study what butterflies normally drink, they don't give nectar to butterflies in a lab. They observe butterflies drinking nectar in the wild.

An experimental study is different. In an experimental study, the scientist systematically gives the participants or subjects a treatment or substance (such as nectar) and records the outcome. Researchers often use a control group in an experiment. The control group does not receive the treatment or substance. The group is a benchmark for comparing to the group that did receive the treatment. Let's say that biologists want to study how a specific kind of nectar affects butterflies. They would give that nectar to one group of butterflies and compare them to the same kind of butterflies that did not get the nectar (the control group). Suppose the butterflies that got the nectar get sick and those that didn't get the nectar remain healthy. That would show that the nectar was likely causing the sickness.

dioxide and other heat-trapping gases to Earth's atmosphere. Humans burn fossil fuels to run cars, machinery, and power plants and to heat and cool buildings. The excess carbon dioxide in the atmosphere is like a blanket, trapping more and more heat from the sun. As a result, temperatures on Earth are increasing. The rising temperatures are changing Earth's weather patterns and creating more extreme weather events. Climate change hurts forests. Many trees cannot adapt to the higher temperatures, extreme weather, and changing rainfall patterns brought by climate change. For example, climate change has brought drought—periods of little or no rainfall—to some areas. Many trees and livestock have died because of insufficient water. Hot weather and little rainfall have led in some places to fierce wildfires, which have destroyed large areas of forest.

LISTEN UP

We need trees and forests to help maintain the cycles that keep our air and water healthy for all life on Earth, and trees need us to protect them from destruction and degradation. The work of biologists, ecologists, foresters, and other scientists is key to this protection.

Trees are both easy and challenging to study. They are easy because they stay in one place. They are challenging because their life spans can be long—often one hundred years or more—outlasting the scientists who study them. Also, scientists can observe some tree processes, such as growth and deforestation, with just their eyes. But to understand other processes, such as how trees take in nutrients and how trees affect human health, scientists often need to design experiments and work in laboratories with advanced scientific techniques and sophisticated machinery.

Have you heard the question "If a tree falls in the forest and no one is there to hear it, does it make a sound?" In fact, trees are making sounds all the time. They communicate with us and with one another. If trees are talking in the forest, on our streets, and in our own backyards, we need to listen. Many scientists are doing just that. You can too.

CHAPTER 1

OUR TREES, OUR LIFE

LIFE ON EARTH IS INCONCEIVABLE WITHOUT TREES.

—Anton Chekhov, nineteenth-century Russian author

We *connect* with trees every day. How? Think of all the things made from trees that you used today. Start with breakfast. Did the fruit you ate or the fruit juice you drank come from a tree? Did you eat any almonds, walnuts, or pecans? These nuts and many others come from trees. Maybe you poured some maple syrup—made from the sap of a maple tree—onto your pancakes. Was your breakfast spicy? Many spices, such as pepper, cinnamon, and clove, come from trees. The containers that held your milk and cereal were probably made of cardboard, which comes from wood pulp (wood that has been pulverized). Are the chair and table where you sat to eat made of wood? Is the floor in your house made of wood planks? Is the house itself built of wood? Did you read a book or newspaper while you ate? Like cardboard, almost all paper is made from wood pulp. Did you practice a musical instrument before you left for school? Most string and wind instruments are made of wood. And that's just the breakfast list. Try making a list of the tree products you use in a full day.

FOREST PHARMACY

In addition to giving us food, shelter, and useful products, trees also provide us with many medicines. One of the most famous medicinal trees is the Pacific yew, which grows in Alaska, Washington, Oregon, and California. The bark of this tree gives us a cancer-fighting substance called paclitaxel. Humans rely on drugs made from tree materials to treat more common ailments as well. For example, the

Several species of yew trees produce paclitaxel, a cancer-fighting substance. Scientists at the Taiwan Forestry Research Institute grow yew trees specifically to extract paclitaxel for medical research.

TREE BASICS

All trees have a trunk, branches, leaves, roots, and bark. Inside, trees contain a vast, microscopic network of tissues called xylem and phloem. Water and minerals travel through xylem from a tree's roots to its leaves. Food made through photosynthesis travels through phloem from leaves to other parts of the tree.

Botanists divide trees into six different groups: broadleaf trees; needleleaf trees; palm, pandanus, and lily trees; cycad trees; tree ferns; and ginkgo trees. The most familiar trees in the United States and other northern nations are broadleaf and needleleaf trees.

Broadleaf trees have flat, wide leaves with veins running through them. Their seeds grow inside fruits. Apple, oak, maple, and birch trees are examples of broadleaf trees. In temperate (mild) climates, most broadleaf trees lose their leaves in fall and winter. They grow new leaves in spring. Trees that lose their leaves each year are called deciduous trees.

Needleleaf trees have needlelike leaves. Most needleleaf trees keep their leaves all year-round, so they are "ever green," which is why we call them evergreens. Needleleaf trees are called coniferous trees because their seeds grow seeds inside cones. (The terms *coniferous* and *conifer* come from the Latin word *conus*, meaning "cone.") Pine, spruce, cedar, and fir trees are examples of coniferous trees.

A tree's life begins when a seed starts to grow. Once the seed has developed a tiny root and stem, it is called a seedling. When the stem grows and leaves form, the seedling becomes a sapling, a very young tree. The sapling continues to grow, developing a woody trunk, branches, leaves, and a root system. It may take many years to become a mature tree that can produce seeds to make new trees.

Inside a tree, water and minerals taken up by the roots move through xylem. Food made in the leaves by photosynthesis travels through phloem.

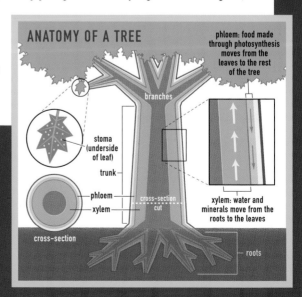

ANATOMY OF A TREE

phloem: food made through photosynthesis moves from the leaves to the rest of the tree

branches

stoma (underside of leaf)

trunk

phloem

xylem

cross-section cut

cross-section

xylem: water and minerals move from the roots to the leaves

roots

bark of willow trees contains a substance called salicin, which is known to reduce pain and fever. For thousands of years, American Indians chewed willow bark for its healing properties.

When modern pharmacologists develop tree-based medicines, they often start by studying how ancient and indigenous (native or local) peoples used tree parts as medicine. They then work in the lab. They extract the healing substance from a tree's bark, wood, or leaves and test its effects, first on lab animals and then on human subjects.

Collecting large amounts of medicine from tree parts can damage and even kill trees. To protect trees, pharmacologists sometimes develop synthetic (laboratory-made) substitutes for the healing chemicals from a tree. In this way, pharmaceutical companies can obtain the medicine without harming trees at the same time. For example, pharmaceutical companies once used salicin from willow trees to make aspirin. Then chemists developed a synthetic form of salicin: acetylsalicylic acid. Modern pharmaceutical companies use this substance to make aspirin. They no longer extract salicin from willow trees.

THE AIR WE BREATHE

Trees also give us oxygen, a gas that almost all living things need. Humans and other animals take in oxygen from the air when they inhale, and they expel the gas carbon dioxide when they exhale. Trees do just the opposite. During the day, they expel oxygen and absorb carbon dioxide. Trees need carbon dioxide to survive.

Trees and other plants absorb carbon dioxide as part of their food-making process: photosynthesis. *Photo* means "light" and *synthesis* means "bringing together." Trees and other plants take in light from the sun, carbon dioxide from the air, and water and other nutrients from the soil and combine them to make glucose, a kind of sugar, which trees and other green plants use as food. This process also releases oxygen, which plants expel through their stomata, tiny holes

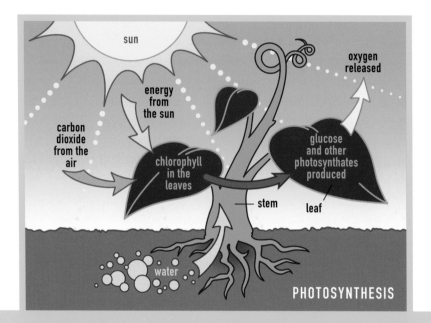

Trees and other plants make food through photosynthesis. During this process, plants release life-giving oxygen. And by absorbing carbon dioxide during photosynthesis, plants reduce atmospheric carbon dioxide levels, which helps in the fight against climate change.

on the undersides of leaves. The process by which trees and other plants release oxygen is called oxygen turnover.

Trees release different amounts of oxygen depending on the type of tree, size of tree, and weather conditions. Big trees in tropical (warm and wet) climates provide more oxygen than trees in other climates. Because trees provide humans with oxygen and humans provide trees with carbon dioxide, scientists say that we are in a symbiotic relationship with trees. That means that the relationship is beneficial to both humans and trees.

RAINMAKERS

Trees are part of Earth's water cycle. In this never-ending cycle, precipitation (rain and snow) falls from clouds. Some of this water falls into lakes, rivers, and oceans. Some of it seeps underground. Trees and other plants take up water from the ground through their roots. They use some of this water to make food during photosynthesis. They also store water in their trunks and leaves. In a process called transpiration, excess water moves through trees and other plants and exits leaves through their stomata. This water takes the form of water vapor— water in gas form. In the air, droplets of water vapor combine with one another to form clouds that precipitate (release) rain and snow. That's how the water cycle continues.

Water also evaporates (turns into water vapor) from the surface of the ocean and other bodies of water. That evaporation creates vast amounts of rain. But evaporation from forests also creates a lot of rain. David Ellison, a researcher with the Institute for World Economics in Budapest, Hungary, says, "Evapo-transpiration [from trees] is a very

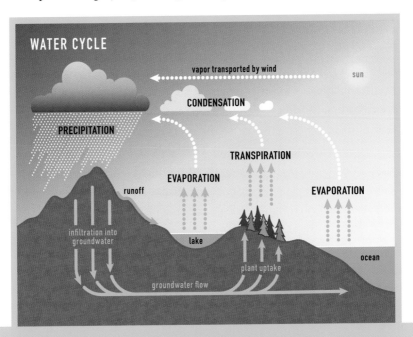

WATER CYCLE

vapor transported by wind

sun

CONDENSATION

PRECIPITATION

TRANSPIRATION

EVAPORATION

EVAPORATION

runoff

infiltration into groundwater

lake

ocean

plant uptake

groundwater flow

Water travels between Earth and the atmosphere in a never-ending cycle. Trees are part of this cycle. They take up water from the soil through their roots and release it into the atmosphere through their leaves.

large component of rain generation—on average about 50% in summer across the globe, and 40% on an annual basis."

Since trees play such a big role in rainfall, it makes sense to plant trees in areas that suffer from drought. In many regions of Africa, including the southern portion of the Sahara and the nation of South Africa, people have planted millions of acres of parched land with new trees. These trees take in water through their roots and release it into the air via transpiration. The result is more rainfall, which in turn helps more trees grow and relieves the pattern of drought.

To encourage rainfall, it also makes sense to maintain existing forests. Forests are fine-tuned instruments that generate and maintain a water supply for their regions. If forests are destroyed, much of our rain will disappear too. To have the water we need, we must preserve the forests we have and find ways to recover the forests we've lost.

CARBON STORAGE EXPERTS

Trees are also part of Earth's carbon cycle. Like water, carbon moves back and forth among the ground, bodies of water, living things, and the atmosphere in a never-ending process. As part of this cycle, trees absorb carbon dioxide, which they use in photosynthesis. They release some of this gas back into the air through their stomata. They also store carbon in their tissues. When a tree dies and decays, the carbon it holds slowly enters the soil and the atmosphere.

In the face of global climate change, trees are more important than ever. For one thing, trees help cool the planet. The water vapor that exits their leaves during transpiration cools the air. Trees also provide shade, which can make our bodies feel 10°F to 15°F (5.6°C to 8°C) cooler than they normally would. Even a small tree can provide as much cooling as two window air conditioners. Trees also shade buildings, reducing air-conditioning costs by as much as 30 percent. Most importantly, trees' ability to store carbon helps fight climate change. The more trees that are growing on Earth,

SOMETHING FISHY

Trees benefit animals as well as people. Monkeys, birds, frogs, snakes, koala bears, lemurs, and insects all make their homes in trees. Believe it or not, even some fish make their homes in trees! The roots of mangrove forests, which grow in shallow water, are home to a large variety of fish, crab, shrimp, and mollusks. When mangrove forests are cut down, these animals lose their homes.

Humans and land animals eat fruits and nuts from trees. Fish get nourishment from trees in another way. When tree leaves decompose, the acids they contain seep into the soil and nearby waterways. In the 1970s, Katsuhiko Matsunaga, a marine chemist at Hokkaido University in Japan, discovered that when these acids seep into the ocean, they help fertilize plankton. Plankton are tiny water organisms that serve as food for many larger animals. When plankton thrive, so do animals that feed on them.

In a campaign called Mori wa Umi no Koibito (Forests Are Lovers of the Sea), people in the Japanese fishing industry plant forests along coasts and rivers to increase nourishment for plankton. This in turn helps feed and increase fish and oyster stocks.

Japanese oyster farmer Shigeatsu Hatakeyama launched Forests Are Lovers of the Sea in 1989. The waters where he had his farm, Kesennuma Bay in Miyagi, Japan, had become unsuitable for oyster cultivation due to an outbreak of red tide (an invasion of toxic algae). With others, Hatakeyama planted broadleaf trees upstream along the Okawa River. The trees added nourishing acids into the water. They also created a shaded, cool environment that attracted microbes and insects that devour pollutants, keeping them from flowing into the sea. Since 1989, Forests Are Lovers of the Sea has planted more than fifty thousand trees. The group does other work to protect the environment, such as promoting farms that do not use harmful pesticides (chemicals that kill insects) and other chemicals.

In 2009 Hatakeyama, whose nickname is Grandpa Oyster, established a Forests Are Lovers of the Sea program for children. It provides hands-on environmental education outdoors. For example, young people taking part in the program plant trees, explore coastlines, and learn about oysters.

Mangrove trees grow along tropical shorelines. Their exposed roots hold the soil in place and protect coastal areas from storm damage.

the more carbon dioxide they absorb. And the more they absorb, the less is in the atmosphere to trap the sun's heat. So Earth stays cooler.

AT THE ROOT

There's much more to a tree than the trunk, branches, and leaves we see aboveground. Tree roots form a deep underground network. This tangle of roots protects the soil by holding it in place and preventing it from washing away during storms or blowing away in high winds—a process known as erosion.

Trees help prevent flooding by intercepting rain in their canopies (uppermost leaves and branches). The water then drops to the ground, seeping slowly into the soil. The water goes to tree roots and into natural underground reservoirs called aquifers—an important source of drinking water and water for farming. Without trees to capture heavy rains, water often floods dry land and overwhelms rivers and storm sewers.

Mangrove trees, which grow along salty ocean shorelines, provide important coastal protection. Their dense root systems help prevent erosion from waves and storms. Humans sometimes clear mangroves for shrimp farming, to build industrial facilities, and for urban development. In areas where mangroves have been cleared, coastal damage from hurricanes and typhoons is much more severe than in places where the mangroves remain untouched.

Tree roots also filter water, making it cleaner. A dense community of microbes living on tree roots traps waterborne substances such as phosphorus, nitrogen, and even toxic wastes. These organisms pull the substances from water and store them in their tissues. The water left behind is cleaner and safer for humans and animals to drink.

CHAPTER 2

HEALTHY TREES, HEALTHY HUMANS

IF YOU GO OFF INTO A FAR, FAR FOREST
AND GET VERY QUIET, YOU'LL COME TO
UNDERSTAND THAT YOU ARE CONNECTED
TO EVERYTHING.

—Alan Watts, twentieth-century British philosopher

Geoffrey Donovan is a researcher at the US Forest Service's Pacific Northwest Research Station in Portland, Oregon. In 2011 he was thinking about the connection between trees and human health. At the time, this connection was well known. A number of studies had shown that tree leaves filter particulate matter (PM, or tiny particles of liquids and solids in the air) from the atmosphere. PM includes dust, pollen, soot, and other materials, some of which are toxic to humans and animals. The Nature Conservancy's *Planting Healthy Air* report found that the average reduction of PM near a tree is between 7 and 24 percent.

Studies show that spending time among trees has a calming effect and can even improve human health.

TREES AND VOCs

The phytoncides that trees release to fight diseases and insects can be beneficial to humans as well. But trees also emit chemicals that—under certain circumstances—can hurt people. These chemicals are called volatile organic compounds (VOCs). VOCs are substances that evaporate at ordinary room temperatures. Another name for this evaporation is outgassing.

VOCs come from many sources besides trees. Some come from petroleum. Manufacturers use others to make paints, household cleaners, and cosmetics. Other VOCs come from human processes, such as the burning of fossil fuels.

Trees emit some types of VOCs to repel insects. They emit other VOCs to attract insects that help them reproduce. (In the process of gathering nectar from flowers, insects carry pollen, or male sex cells, to a tree's female reproductive organs. The merging of male and female reproductive cells creates seeds, from which new trees grow.) Tree species such as birch, tulip, and linden release very low levels of VOCs. Other trees, such as black gum, poplar, oak, and willow, release high levels of VOCs. The Great Smoky Mountains in the southern United States are called "smoky" because the trees there give off large amounts of VOCs.

The VOCs from petroleum products include dangerous chemicals such as benzene, which can cause cancer in humans. The VOCs from trees, such as terpenes (used to make turpentine) and isoprene (used to make rubber), do not on their own pose much danger to human health. Even the many VOCs given off by trees in the Great Smoky Mountains are not harmful to humans. The threat comes when large amounts of VOCs, from trees and other sources, combine with sunlight and nitrogen oxides (a group of air pollutants released by the burning of fossil fuels) to create ozone.

High in the atmosphere, ozone protects living things by blocking harmful rays from the sun. But at ground level, ozone is dangerous. It can make breathing difficult, can cause coughing and sore throat, can aggravate asthma and other lung diseases, and can lead to long-term respiratory illness. The solution to the dangers of VOCs is not to avoid trees or to plant fewer trees. The solution is to reduce the amount of nitrogen oxides and petroleum-based VOCs in the atmosphere. The result will be less ozone at ground level to threaten human health.

While particulate matter does not harm trees, it can damage human health. When people inhale particles from toxic chemical emissions, for example, the PM can lodge in the lungs and cause cardiovascular and respiratory diseases, including asthma and bronchitis. Some PM can lead to lung cancers. Research shows that high concentrations of particulate matter cause more than three million premature deaths worldwide every year. Conversely, less air pollution translates into better human health. For instance, a 2008 study by researchers at Columbia University in New York City found that more trees in urban neighborhoods correlate with (have a connection to but are not necessarily responsible for) a lower incidence of asthma.

The World Health Organization (WHO) is an international agency dedicated to monitoring, protecting, and improving human health. WHO sets standards for clean air. Studies of urban areas have found that more than 80 percent of the people living in London, England; Tokyo, Japan; Los Angeles, California; Mexico City, Mexico; Beijing, China; and other big cities are exposed to air pollution levels that exceed the limits WHO believes to be safe.

Geoffrey Donovan knew that trees could help. In addition to capturing harmful material from the air, trees release beneficial chemical substances through their leaves and trunks. These airborne chemicals, called phytoncides, protect trees from insects and help trees fight diseases carried by bacteria and fungi. Studies have shown that inhaling phytoncides can even help human health. In humans, inhaled phytoncides increase the number and activity of white blood cells called natural killer cells. These cells kill tumor- and virus-infected cells in our bodies.

QUESTION AND ANSWERS

Donovan realized, "If having trees is good for you, the opposite must also be true: not having trees is bad for you." Donovan kept thinking. One day, while daydreaming during a meeting, he got the idea for his study. Looking out the window at a barren landscape, a question popped into his head: "What becomes of people's health when trees die?" That became his guiding research question.

Once he had his question, he needed to find relevant data. Donovan knew that starting in 2002, the emerald ash borer—a beetle that's smaller than a penny—had begun to infest millions of ash trees throughout North America. Adult beetles lay their eggs on ash trees. Larvae (immature forms of insects) hatch from the eggs, bore into the bark, and feed on tissue that transports nutrients and water to feed the tree. In this way, the larvae make it impossible for a tree to get the substances it needs to live. By 2012 emerald ash borer larvae had killed more than one hundred million trees.

> ## "WE'VE HAD THIS INTUITIVE UNDERSTANDING THAT NATURE IS GOOD FOR US. NOW WE'RE BACKING IT UP [WITH DATA]."
>
> **—Geoffrey Donovan**

Donovan set up an experiment to find out if living in places where ash trees had died correlated with people having poor health. He said, "I knew if I found something, it was going to be important."

Donovan compared human deaths in areas where ash trees had died to those where the trees hadn't died, using the five-year period from 2002 to 2007. To find the number of ash tree deaths, he consulted the Animal and Plant Health Inspection Service (APHIS), part of the US Department of Agriculture. APHIS tracks the emerald ash borer and how many trees it kills. Donovan used data on human deaths collected by the National Center for Health Statistics, a US government agency. He also collaborated with experts in other fields, including a statistician, an epidemiologist (a scientist who studies how diseases behave in human populations), an entomologist (a scientist who studies insects), and a forest ecologist who specialized in satellite imagery technology. They helped design the study, collect the data, and analyze it.

Donovan also wrote and entered computer code to help with analyzing the data. The research took many months. All that time and energy paid off. When Donovan began to run the data through his computer software, he started to see intriguing relationships and connections. For example, Donovan saw that between 2002 and 2007, places with emerald ash borer infestations had fifteen thousand more deaths from cardiovascular (heart) disease and six thousand more deaths from lower-respiratory disease than places with no infestations. He noticed that the deaths of the infested ash trees followed a specific geographic pattern. And the increased cases of cardiovascular disease and lower-respiratory disease followed a similar pattern.

The findings suggest that emerald ash borers and other tree pests may pose a significant public health threat. And living near healthy trees may protect people against cardiovascular and respiratory diseases. While Donovan can't say that the lack of trees caused people's health issues, the evidence he found shows a strong correlation.

THE FEEL-GOOD FACTOR

As it turns out, trees don't just make people physically healthier. They also improve our spiritual well-being. One of the first researchers to study the effect of trees on health was Roger Ulrich, a professor of architecture and health-care facility design at the University of Delaware. In 1984 he shared an important discovery: seeing trees could make hospital patients heal more quickly—and with fewer painkillers.

SCIENTIST PROFILE: GEOFFREY DONOVAN

Growing up in Yorkshire, England, Geoffrey Donovan enjoyed playing outdoors. He climbed rocks and trees, but he was clumsy and fell down frequently. He spent a lot of time in the emergency room, where doctors treated his bumps, bruises, and broken bones.

In between emergency room visits, he enjoyed mathematics and science in high school and college in England, and when he moved to the United States for graduate school at Colorado State University. He steered clear of the sciences that involved a lot of laboratory work, such as chemistry and physics. He found that he was too clumsy to carry out precision laboratory experiments. He limited his physical activities to his free time and decided to pursue economics and data research in forestry as a career. He's pretty safe from breaking any bones while exploring economics and forestry data. But he still hurts himself regularly having fun outdoors.

In addition to working for the US Forest Service, Donovan teaches urban forestry at Portland State University in Oregon. He encourages his students to leave their biases and egos out of the work and focus on the research methods. He says, "It's not about you and your beliefs. What's important are the questions and the answers you can provide." He also encourages his students to look to the data for the facts rather than relying on their opinions of the natural world. He asks them to consider, "How do you know what's factual and what isn't? Enough of opinions. Let's try to find out the facts."

Donovan says that a "great thing about scientific research is you choose who you work with on different studies. I get to work with great people over and over again." He also enjoys getting "paid to be curious and given the freedom to follow his curiosity." And it's exciting when all

the hard work pays off. "It takes a lot of effort looking under all those rocks [doing research]. It's definitely delayed gratification, but it is a sweet moment when that analysis reveals those relationships."

Donovan left Oregon in 2017 for many months to work with the Centre for Public Health Research in Wellington, New Zealand. There he researched how the natural environment affects children and whether trees can reduce the harmful effects of human exposure to pesticides. He also researches how trees affect specific health conditions, including childhood asthma, attention deficit hyperactivity disorder (ADHD), and recovery from surgery.

Trees in urban areas provide shade, trap particulate matter, and help reduce stress in city dwellers.

A hiker walks along a forest trail in Fiordland National Park on New Zealand's South Island. Another name for walking in the woods is *shinrin-yoku*, which means "forest bathing" in Japanese.

His study was small. It included only forty-six gallbladder surgery patients at one hospital. The patients who could see trees outside their hospital room window stayed in the hospital for less time than the patients who had windows that faced a brick wall. Ulrich's research opened up a new field of investigation: What do trees do for human health by our seeing or being near them? What communication is happening between humans and trees?

Since Ulrich's discovery, more researchers have studied the effects of trees and forests on human physical and mental health.

In the early 1990s, the Japanese Ministry of Agriculture, Forestry and Fisheries coined the term *shinrin-yoku*, which means "forest bathing." Studies show that forest bathing—a walk in the woods, using all the senses to take in the surroundings—alters the body's chemistry. It reduces stress and blood pressure. In 2015 researchers at Stanford University in California found that just a fifty-minute walk in a park or forest could decrease anxiety and negative thoughts. The researchers found that a fifty-minute walk through an urban environment had no such helpful effect. However, studies of inner cities in the United States show that walking among trees in a city does reduce anxiety and depression. "We've had this intuitive understanding that nature is good for us," said Geoffrey Donovan. "Now we're backing it up [with data]."

HEALTHY TREES, HEALTHY HUMANS

CHAPTER 3

TREES TALK TO ONE ANOTHER

WHEN YOU KNOW THAT TREES EXPERIENCE PAIN AND HAVE MEMORIES, AND THAT TREE PARENTS LIVE TOGETHER WITH THEIR CHILDREN, THEN YOU CAN NO LONGER JUST CHOP THEM DOWN AND DISRUPT THEIR LIVES WITH LARGE MACHINES.

—German forester Peter Wohlleben, in *The Hidden Life of Trees*, 2016

Douglas fir and paper birch trees are talking to each other in the forest! An experiment in 1997 led Suzanne Simard to this discovery. "At that moment, everything came into focus for me. I knew I had found something big, something that would change the way we look at how trees interact in forests," says Simard, a professor of forest ecology at the University of British Columbia in Vancouver, Canada. In her study of paper birch, Douglas fir, and western red cedar trees, Simard found evidence of a massive belowground communication network of fungi and roots that trees use to communicate with one another. She had found another world.

Everything in a forest is connected. Dead, decaying trees provide nourishment for fungi, insects, and other forest organisms. Animals make their homes among tree roots, stumps, and branches.

THE FOUR FUNGI

Mycorrhizal fungus is one of four categories of fungi. The others are saprophytic, parasitic, and endophytic fungi. Fungi are categorized based on how they feed themselves.

Saprophytic fungi are decomposers. When forest plants and animals die, saprophytic fungi break down and eat their remains. The dead matter nourishes the fungi, enabling them to grow and reach more parts of the forest floor. Bacteria and other invertebrates (animals without backbones), such as worms, slugs, and snails, feed on the dead material too. The fungi and other creatures extract all the food they can from the dead matter. What is left behind is humus, a nutrient-rich soil.

Parasitic fungi don't wait for living things to die and fall to the forest floor. These predators take their nourishment from living plants and animals. (Parasites are living things that feed off other living things.) Some parasitic fungi kill the creatures they live on. An example is the honey fungus, which feeds on the roots of trees and woody shrubs. The fungus spreads underground, although you can see its mushrooms (fleshy fruit) growing aboveground in the fall. The honey fungus causes plant roots to rot and often kills the whole plant.

Like mycorrhizal fungi, endophytic fungi are in a symbiotic relationship with trees. The tree shares nutrients with the fungi. In return, the fungi enhance the tree's growth by increasing its ability to absorb nutrients. These common fungi enter and live in the cells of the tree without causing harm to the tree.

German forester Peter Wohlleben uses a section of soil enclosed in glass to teach about underground mycorrhizal networks.

THERE'S A FUNGUS AMONG US!

Dig down deep into the soft, dark brown soil. It crumbles into chunks like moist chocolate cake. As the nutrient-rich soil falls away, you see the tree roots encased in what look like cobwebs. These fuzzy white threads are actually fungi. Peter Wohlleben, a German forester and author of *The Hidden Life of Trees*, found that "a mere teaspoonful [of soil] contains many miles of fungal filaments." These filaments and the tree roots they surround have a symbiotic relationship. In this relationship, the roots give carbon from the plant to the fungi and the fungi supply water and minerals from the soil to the roots. This relationship helps both fungi and trees grow and thrive.

A symbiotic association between a fungus and the roots of a tree or other plant is called a mycorrhiza. Fungi that have such relationships are called mycorrhizal fungi. The word *mycorrhiza* comes from two Greek words: *myco* means "fungus" and *rhiza* means "root."

In a mycorrhizal network, a single tree may be physically linked to hundreds of trees as well as to other plants. Forest ecologists call this network of trees the Wood Wide Web because it is similar in structure to the World Wide Web. In cyberspace, the web encompasses all the interactions between humans and the millions of networked computers that make up the internet.

Scientists have been looking at mycorrhizal associations since the nineteenth century. In 1885 German botanist Albert B. Frank wrote a paper about the symbiotic relationship between fungi and plants. In the 1980s, biologists at various institutions documented which fungi species and which tree species were associated in mycorrhizal relationships. The researchers found that some fungi associate with only certain trees, while others are generalists that can associate with many tree species.

In the early 1990s, Suzanne Simard was studying for her PhD in forest sciences at Oregon State University. She learned that in laboratory experiments, biologists had discovered that via a mycorrhizal network, one pine seedling root could transmit carbon to another pine seedling root. Simard wondered if this transmission could happen outside the laboratory, in real forests. She had noticed that when loggers removed paper birch trees from a forest, Douglas fir trees in the same area often died. Simard suspected that the trees were sharing resources and information belowground through a mycorrhizal network.

Not all researchers agreed with Simard's idea. They did not believe trees were connected. Some people said she was foolish for suggesting that trees communicate with one another. Because other scientists were not convinced Simard had a good idea, she had a hard time getting funding for her research. She was unable to get money from government organizations, private foundations, and other groups that normally fund scientific research. Simard persisted. She felt passionate about understanding the relationships among trees. She decided to keep doing her research despite the lack of money and the naysayers.

MAKING THE DISCOVERY

In the mid-1990s, Simard conducted experiments in the forests of British Columbia. She grew eighty trees of three species—paper birch, Douglas fir, and western red cedar—together in specific areas of the forest. She believed that the paper birch and Douglas fir trees were connected belowground but that the red cedar trees did not share the same fungal network. She wanted to see whether trees passed the carbon they absorbed during photosynthesis to one another through their roots.

Simard prepared syringes full of radioactive carbon-14 gas and nonradioactive carbon-13 gas. She would inject these gases into trees and detect their movement using a Geiger counter, an instrument that detects radiation. She borrowed the Geiger counter from her university. She bought plastic bags, duct tape, shade cloth, a timer, a white paper suit, and a respirator to cover her nose and mouth so she wouldn't breathe in any of the harmful radioactive carbon used in her experiment.

On the first day of her experiment in the forest, a grizzly bear and her cub chased Simard away from the trees she had planted. She returned the next day—no bears in sight—and got started. She put on her white paper suit, put on her respirator, and then put plastic bags over a birch tree and a fir tree.

She injected radioactive carbon-14 into the bag covering the birch tree. She injected nonradioactive carbon-13 into the bag around the fir tree. She wanted to find out whether the two different types of trees were sharing carbon. She also put a shade cloth over the fir tree. The shade cloth kept sunlight from reaching the fir tree. Without light, the tree could not carry out photosynthesis and therefore could not take in carbon from the atmosphere. The fir tree would need extra carbon, and Simard wondered whether it would get some from the birch tree.

Just as Simard was finishing this portion of the experiment, the mama grizzly returned! The bear chased Simard, who ran, swatting mosquitoes with one hand and holding the syringes above her head in the other hand. She made it to her truck, jumped in, and thought, "This is why people do lab studies."

She sat in her truck, waiting for the bear to leave but also waiting for the trees to absorb the extra carbon, turn it into glucose, and—if her ideas about trees sharing carbon proved correct—send it through their roots to one another. After an hour had passed, she checked for the bear. All clear.

She got out of the truck and went to the birch tree. She pulled the bag off and ran the Geiger counter over its leaves. She heard a *kkhh!* sound. The Geiger counter indicated that the birch had taken up the radioactive carbon-14 gas. Next, she went to the fir tree. She pulled off its bag and ran the Geiger counter up its needles. Again, she heard *kkhh!* This meant that the fir tree had also taken up radioactive carbon-14 gas. Simard hadn't injected the fir trees with carbon-14 gas, so it had to have come from the birch tree. Simard says that the sound of the Geiger counter was sort of like the sound of the birch and fir tree talking to each other. The birch was saying, "Hey, can I help you? And the fir was saying, Yeah, can you send me some of your carbon? Because somebody threw a shade cloth over me," so I can't use sunlight to carry out photosynthesis and I can't absorb carbon. Finally, she checked on a cedar tree, which she had not covered with a bag or injected with carbon gas. She ran the Geiger counter over its leaves. Silence. The cedar was in its own world. It had not taken in any of the carbon-14 gas. It was not connected to the web that linked the birch and fir.

Simard wrote up her experiment for her dissertation (a research paper required for anyone graduating with a PhD). *Nature*, a scientific journal, published part of her dissertation in 1997. Her discovery that trees communicate with one another rocked the world. Journalists and other scientists read about her work. They began translating it into foreign languages and publishing it in other journals and in textbooks.

The white fibers in this photograph are mycorrhizal fungi. Part of the Wood Wide Web, the fungi surround tree roots and pass carbon, water, minerals, and other substances along the network.

Once she had figured out that birch trees and fir trees were sharing carbon, Simard wanted to determine *why* they were sharing it—in the real world and not just in the context of her experiment. She explains that in summer, Douglas fir seedlings don't get much sunlight because broadleaf trees fill the forest canopy. The leaves in the canopy absorb most of the sunlight before it reaches the forest floor. Without sunlight, fir seedlings cannot practice photosynthesis or take in the carbon they desperately need. Paper birch trees, on the other hand, grow high in the sun-drenched forest canopy. They take in plenty of sunlight for photosynthesis and absorb lots of carbon. They have extra carbon to share with the Douglas fir seedlings. During fall and winter, the situation is reversed. The

TREES TALK TO ONE ANOTHER

SCIENTIST PROFILE: SUZANNE SIMARD

Suzanne Simard comes from a family of loggers. More than one hundred years ago, her ancestors logged the forests of British Columbia. Simard Mountain in British Columbia is named for one of these ancestors. As a child, Simard spent a lot of time in forests. She would lie on the forest floor and stare up at the treetops. She loved playing in the forest, watching the bugs. She was fascinated with the forest soil. She loved observing how soil animals, such as worms and ants, interacted with trees. Her grandpa taught her to experience the peacefulness of the woods and the forest community.

One day, Jigs, the family dog, slipped and fell into an outhouse pit. Simard and her grandpa rushed to rescue him from the muck. Her grandpa grabbed a shovel. As he dug through the forest floor adjacent to the mucky pit, Simard watched, fascinated. Her grandpa's shovel exposed roots, mycorrhizal fungi, and under that red and yellow minerals. Eventually, she and her grandpa rescued Jigs. In the process, she discovered the pallet of roots and soil that is the foundation of the forest.

As a professor of forest ecology, Simard continues to investigate biodiversity, climate change, conservation, ecology, ecosystems, forest biology, forest management, microbiology, soil science, and mycorrhizal networks. Just like trees, these areas of science are interconnected. Between 2011 and 2016, Simard led TerreWEB. This program at the University of British Columbia trained graduate students and postgraduate

deciduous paper birch trees have lost their leaves, so they can't practice photosynthesis or absorb carbon. The Douglas fir trees now have plenty of carbon, because with their evergreen needles, they photosynthesize year-round. So the Douglas fir returns the favor,

professionals how best to convey their climate change research findings to audiences, using TV, film, the internet, and other media. Simard also shares her own research through a variety of media, including TEDx Talks (short presentations by experts), film, videos, journal articles, and books.

Some of Suzanne Simard's ancestors were loggers in British Columbia. This photo from around 1900 shows loggers surrounded by felled trees, tree stumps, and oxen that will haul the logs to a lumber mill near Vancouver, British Columbia.

providing the leafless paper birch with carbon. Simard elaborates, "One of the important things that we tested in [our] experiment was shading. The more Douglas fir became shaded in the summertime, the more excess carbon [that] the birch had went to the fir. Then later

TREES TALK TO ONE ANOTHER

in the fall, when the birch was losing its leaves and the fir had excess carbon because it was still photosynthesizing, the net transfer of this exchange went back to the birch."

Since Simard's big discovery, she, her students, and other researchers have conducted additional studies on mycorrhizal networks. Their research has shown that trees share not only carbon but also water and nutrients such as nitrogen and phosphorus. And trees don't just transfer resources. They also send electrical currents and chemicals to help other trees defend themselves against predators and disease.

NO FUNGUS, NO FOREST

Even though we don't see it, the Wood Wide Web makes healthy forests possible. All plants in a forest, including trees, connect to this network. These connections began a long time ago. In fact, scientists have found fossilized mycorrhizal fungi dating back four hundred million years.

Mycorrhizal fungi strengthen and support plant health. For example, these fungi are decomposer superstars. When forest plants and animals die, fungi help digest their remains, converting them into nutrient-rich soil. Mycorrhizal fungi also access water that trees cannot reach with their roots and deliver it to trees. They even redistribute water among trees on the network.

Botanists have found that connecting to a mycorrhizal network also helps trees defend themselves from predators, such as insects. When trees are under attack, first, they protect themselves. For example, when a beetle or caterpillar starts nibbling on a tree's leaves, the tree sends distress signals throughout its body. The signals take the form of electrical current. The current travels slowly throughout the tree—at the rate of one-third of an inch (0.8 cm) per minute. It may take an hour for the signals to reach all the leaves. The leaves then make and release toxins, turning the insects' delicious feast into inedible foliage. After defending itself, a tree that is under attack might also send signals to its neighbors. Some trees send chemical signals

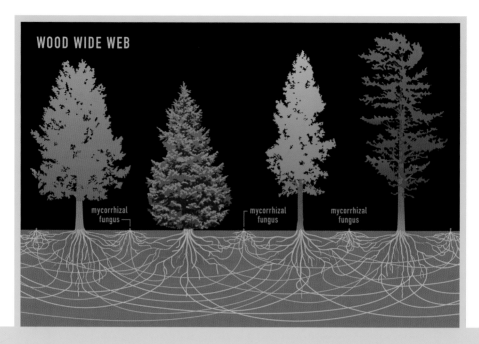

WOOD WIDE WEB

mycorrhizal fungus

mycorrhizal fungus

mycorrhizal fungus

The Wood Wide Web is an extensive underground network. This web allows trees to share resources, and the healthiest trees have the most connections.

through the air. Others send them through mycorrhizal networks, alerting other trees that insects are attacking or perhaps that giraffes are in the area, munching on leaves. A tree that receives the signal can increase its own chemical defenses, so when the giraffes reach it, its leaves have already produced nasty chemicals to repel them.

Finally, mycorrhizal fungi also store carbon, which the network can send to trees that need it. When trees die, some of their carbon enters the soil—and the network. This extra carbon can travel through the network to living trees. In this way, with the passing of carbon from dead trees to living ones, mycorrhizal networks help forests regenerate.

WHO'S TALKING TO WHOM?

Most tree species are connected to many different kinds of fungi on the web. Some fungi are connected to only one species of tree, but

FUNGI ON MY MIND

When foresters set out to preserve, regenerate, diversify, and strengthen forests, they often use their knowledge of the benefits provided by mycorrhizal and other fungi. For example, instead of removing trees that fall in a forest, foresters allow the dead trees to remain on the forest floor, where saprophytic fungi and other organisms can decompose them. This process creates humus, which provides nutrients to other plants. When foresters replant forests, they often use soil that already contains mycorrhizal fungi. The established mycorrhizal networks provide water, carbon, nutrients, and other benefits to the new trees.

Some types of fungi can even clean up polluted areas. Biologists have discovered that certain fungi species produce enzymes (substances that speed up chemical reactions) that absorb and break down pollutants such as toxic chemicals, heavy metals, petroleum, and even plastic and nuclear waste. The pollutants don't hurt the fungi. In 2007 biologists and ecologists launched the Amazon Mycorenewal Project, which uses fungi to clean up pits filled with toxic sludge in northeastern Ecuador. The waste is left over from oil-drilling operations carried out by the Texaco company in the late twentieth century. Another group is using radiation-loving mushrooms to clean up polluted soil around the Fukushima nuclear power plant in Japan. The plant was damaged by an earthquake and tsunami in 2011, and deadly radioactive material contaminated the plant and surrounding areas. Both cleanup projects operate on a small scale. Biologists hope to learn more about pollution-loving fungi, to grow them in large numbers, and to use them to clean up larger areas after oil spills and other human-made disasters.

other fungi are generalists that can form networks among multiple tree species. Trees on the same fungi network can talk to one another but not to those on a different network.

Thousands of mycorrhizal fungi have relationships with trees. The list below includes a few well-known tree and fungi connections:

MYCORRHIZAL FUNGI	TREES ON THE NETWORK
Glomus intraradices	Cedar, redwoods
Pisolithus tinctorius	Pines
Rhizopogon parksii	Deciduous trees
Cantharellus cibarius	Oaks, firs

MOTHER TREES

Suzanne Simard describes mycorrhizal webs as "complex systems with hubs and networks." Hubs are trees on a network that have the most connections and send the most resources to other trees. Also called nodes, or mother trees, they are larger and older than the trees around them. Because they are large, they've got more carbon flowing into them from the atmosphere. They also have more roots to take up water from the soil. In other words, they have more to share with other trees. And because they have more roots, they are connected to more fungi on the network. By contrast, small trees are not linked to as many other trees.

Mother trees help other trees on their networks by sending them carbon, nutrients, and water. If a particular tree is undernourished or unhealthy, a mother tree will send it extra resources. Because mother trees nurture many other trees, when human loggers remove mother trees, they do harm to all the trees connected to mothers on the network.

BRINGING UP BABY

When foresters plant trees to establish or add to a forest, they focus on biodiversity, or having a variety of tree species. Biodiversity in trees and plants is a good thing. It helps a forest survive. Suppose a tree or plant species in a forest becomes infested with insects or disease and dies off. Other species in the forest might have built-in resistance to the same disease or effective defenses against the insects. So those species survive the infestation or the disease. The forest hasn't been completely wiped out. But if a forest has only one species, an infestation could kill off the forest completely.

While biodiversity is important, so are kin relationships—family connections between trees of the same species. In the animal world, mothers take care of their children, and close relatives, such as siblings, look out for one another. The same is true on the Wood Wide Web.

ABOVEGROUND SIGNALS

Trees don't communicate only through the Wood Wide Web. They also produce chemicals that travel through the air, up to 100 feet (30 m) away. These signals might warn other trees that predators are invading so that they can prepare their own defense mechanisms.

Another clever trick: some trees and plants give off a scent that attracts predators of an attacking insect. For example, when beetles start eating wild lima bean plants, the plants release a chemical that attracts beetle-eating spiders and insects. These predators detect the scent and arrive to feast on the beetles eating the plant's leaves.

Some trees send out toxic chemicals that harm other plants. The American black walnut tree is one such species. This tree can inhibit the growth of and even kill other trees and plants by releasing a chemical called juglone from its leaves, bark, and roots. By destroying nearby plants, the American black walnut gets more light, nutrients, water, and space for itself.

Biologists have observed that mother trees send more carbon and chemical signals to their children (their seedlings) and to their siblings (trees that grew from seeds from the same parent plant) than to nonrelated trees. Related trees are healthier and more resistant to disease than those without nearby relatives because they help one another out.

FRIENDSHIPS

Even if they are not siblings or are not from the same species, trees still form relationships with one another on the Wood Wide Web. Why do nonrelated trees help one another out? Because it is the community of the forest that makes it possible for trees to thrive for hundreds of years.

Collectively, a forest can create a climate that helps it adjust to heat, cold, and wind. For example, hundreds or thousands of trees in a forest can all store water in their roots and trunks. Through transpiration, any excess water exits their leaves and turns into water vapor. High in the atmosphere, the water vapor condenses (turns back into liquid water) and falls to the ground as rain or snow. The larger the forest, the more precipitation it can generate, and this provides life-giving water to the forest ecosystem. A large forest—with an extensive canopy of leaves—can also shade the plants and animals living close to the forest floor. This shade keeps a forest cool even in hot weather. Trees in a large forest will also withstand strong winds better than a single tree or just a few trees. For example, a strong windstorm might easily topple a tree standing all by itself. But if that tree is surrounded by hundreds of others, they will protect it from ferocious winds.

Some trees do not have the benefits of being on a strong mycorrhizal network. For instance, logging companies (which operate tree plantations to harvest wood) often plant trees in long rows with wide gaps between them. The big spaces between the trees make it easier for loggers to cut them for timber. Although these widely spaced trees might connect with one another underground, the network is not nearly as extensive or complex as it is in a natural forest. Trees planted in cities—for example, along sidewalks—also can't connect to strong mycorrhizal networks. Without the benefits provided by a network, these trees do not live very long. In fact, trees that are planted as individuals—such as those in cities—live an average of seven years. Trees that are part of the forest community can live to be hundreds of years old.

LIFE AFTER DEATH

The stumps of trees that have fallen or been cut down may appear dead. But a closer look reveals that many are still green, nourished by their friends and kin. Roots of tree stumps connected to other trees through

At a tree farm, cottonwood trees grow in evenly spaced rows, with lots of distance between them. Loggers will cut down the trees to make paper. Because they grow far apart, these trees have fewer mycorrhizal connections and are therefore not as healthy as closely spaced trees.

mycorrhizal networks may receive nutrients from other trees for decades. Why? It appears that relationships die hard. Tree stumps connected to the network may live for many years and might even reproduce. This isn't sexual reproduction—in which a tree's male reproductive cells fertilize its female reproductive cells or those of another tree, resulting in the creation of seeds. Instead, in a type of asexual reproduction, the cells of a living stump divide and form buds that grow to become new trees. Meanwhile, tree stumps that are not connected to a mycorrhizal network will quickly die after they fall or are cut down.

Dead trees stay connected to the forest ecosystem in other ways as well. After a tree dies and falls to the ground, it can take centuries to completely decay. As they lie on the forest floor, the fallen trunk and branches provide nutrition and shelter for whole communities, including mosses, tree seedlings, fungi, small mammals, amphibians, and insects. And the soil around a fallen or cut tree still contains fungal networks that provide nutrients to other plants. So the cycle of life continues in the forest.

CHAPTER 4

THE FOREST CANOPY'S CRY FOR HELP

THE TREE IS MORE THAN FIRST A SEED, THEN
A STEM, THEN A LIVING TRUNK, AND THEN
DEAD TIMBER. THE TREE IS A SLOW, ENDURING
FORCE STRAINING TO WIN THE SKY.

—Antoine de Saint-Exupery, *The Wisdom of the Sands*, 1948

In June 1981, Nalini Nadkarni was right where she loved to be: climbing in the canopy of the deciduous and coniferous trees in the Hoh River Valley, in Olympic National Park in Washington State. This rain forest provides a home to hundreds of plants, insects, and animals. On this summer day, Nadkarni, then a graduate student at the University of Washington in Seattle, made a startling discovery: she found thick mats of roots beneath mosses growing on tree trunks and branches.

Mosses have no roots. And the roots Nadkarni saw weren't the roots of ferns and other plants that grow on trees. She was puzzled. She asked, "What are these roots?" Her discovery of roots

Biology professor Nalini Nadkarni dangles from a rope in a forest canopy in Monteverde, Costa Rica. She and other canopy researchers study the plants, animals, and insects that make their homes in treetops, high above the forest floor.

in the forest canopy made the cover of *Science* magazine in 1981. It awakened the scientific community to the fact that the forest canopy holds unknown ecosystems.

MAKING THE DISCOVERY

Nadkarni made her discovery when she was trying to answer some basic questions about plant life in the forest canopy. She was studying epiphytes, plants that grow on the surface of other plants and that get the moisture and nutrients they need from rain, water vapor in the air, and decaying plant material. Some mosses, orchids, and ferns are epiphytes. Many epiphytes get access to sunlight for photosynthesis by living high in the forest canopy—on the trunks and branches of tall trees. These were the epiphytes Nadkarni studied.

One day she was chopping mosses from trees so she could weigh them when she noticed soil under the mosses. She peeled the soil back

A layer of moss grows on the trunk of a fir tree. Mosses are epiphytes, plants that grow on the surface of other plants and take their nutrients from the air and from rain. Many mosses grow high in the forest canopy.

and, to her surprise, found roots. She wondered what roots were doing in the canopy. Which plants did they belong to? It looked like the roots were growing from the trees themselves. Could a tree have roots in places other than the base of its trunk?

She took her observations and questions back to one of her professors. He said, "What roots in the canopy? There are no roots." So she went back to the forest and checked different types of trees. Every moss bed she lifted had roots beneath it. She was still puzzled. So she checked more than two hundred trees within 20 square miles (52 sq. km), writing down her findings as she went.

To show her professor that the roots really existed, she rented a chain saw, cut out a portion of a tree branch with moss, hauled it in to her professor's office, and said, "These roots!" She showed him her notes, making it clear that she had found the roots on nearly all trees with moss. He said, "This is new stuff. They are roots, and I don't know why they are there or what they are doing."

Next, Nadkarni tried to find out if anyone else knew about these roots. She read what other researchers had written about the same mosses and the trees they grew on to find mention of the roots. Nothing. She contacted experts in roots around the world. Nothing.

INVESTIGATION

It was time for Nadkarni to learn more. First, she wanted to learn if the roots in the tree functioned. That is, did they carry nutrients and water to the tree?

She learned about a technology called gamma spectrometry. With gamma spectrometry, researchers inject radioactive elements into plants or animals in tiny doses. The elements emit a type of radiation called gamma rays. The radiation does not hurt the organisms. Using a gamma spectrometer, a device that measures gamma rays, researchers can trace where the elements travel within the organism. Medical technicians also use this approach to trace blood moving through the human body. Botanists use it to trace how water moves through a tree's circulatory system. Gamma spectrometry helps scientists see what they cannot otherwise observe with their eyes. Nadkarni realized that with gamma spectrometry, she could trace nutrients moving inside a tree, from the roots to the leaves. She could use the technology to determine whether the roots she had found beneath mosses in the rain forest canopy were carrying nutrients to the trees.

At a scientific meeting in 1987, Nadkarni met Richard Primack, a professor of biology at Boston University, who used gamma spectrometry at his laboratory. She spent three weeks in Primack's lab running tests on roots using gamma spectrometry. She and Primack discovered that, yes, the roots in the canopy were functional. They were collecting nutrients from soil accumulating under moss growing on rain forest trees.

SCIENTIST PROFILE: NALINI NADKARNI

Nalini Nadkarni grew up in Bethesda, Maryland, with four siblings. As a child, she spent a lot of time climbing trees in her backyard, playing in the woods, and dancing. With her younger brother, she also enjoyed playing in her family's treehouse and inventing new things—including a skateboard with a sail and a little boat made out of empty milk cartons.

She went to Brown University, where she studied biology and modern dance. After graduating, she spent two years overseas. The first year, she worked as a field biologist in a remote area of Papua New Guinea, an island nation in the southwestern Pacific Ocean. The second year, she lived in Paris, France, learning and performing modern dance. Her graduate degree, from the University of Washington, is in forest ecology—the scientific study of how living organisms relate to one another and to their surroundings in a forest.

The cyclical, systematic nature of the forest appeals to Nadkarni. For example, leaves from trees fall to the forest floor, and as the leaves decay, they turn into humus. Other trees take up the nutrients in the humus through their roots. Nadkarni says, "If you could follow a single atom of nitrogen, from leaf to ground to soil to nutrients taken up by the roots of another tree, you would see the forest is not a static [nonchanging] place with trees standing around. The forest is kind of a dance of energy and materials: carbon and nutrients moving from the canopy to the floor and back up into the canopy. Very dynamic."

Nadkarni has devoted much of her career to communicating what she's learned about the forest canopy to nonscientists, including artists,

musicians, urban youth, legislators, and even prison inmates. She says, "Scientists communicate their findings so we all can break through the wall of ignorance we have about the natural world."

SHARING THE MESSAGE

In 2004, while she was a professor at Evergreen State College in Washington State, Nadkarni cofounded the Evergreen State College and Washington State Department of Corrections Sustainability in Prisons Project. In this program, prison inmates grow gardens, learn about energy conservation, assist in recycling efforts, and do other Earth-friendly work. The project has positively impacted the self-esteem of many inmates, reducing their stress and improving their confidence. "We are trying to create a better world. Whether it is for people or nature, that's really what these projects are about," Nadkarni says.

She uses a variety of media to share her message: books, articles, TED Talks, and even bumper stickers. One bumper sticker seen frequently around the state of Washington says, "Got Oxygen? Thank a Tree." The International Canopy Network, an environmental education organization that Nadkarni founded, prints the bumper stickers.

When Nadkarni first told her professors about roots in the forest canopy, some of them didn't believe her. They said, "No, it's just Tarzan and Jane stuff [not serious]. Stop being silly." Nadkarni went on to become a professor of biology at the University of Utah in Salt Lake City. When her graduate students come to her, she listens. She knows it takes someone saying "I'm not going to follow what everyone else is doing [but I'm going to] try something different" to make important scientific discoveries.

This discovery led to more questions. Where did the soil come from? Answer: decaying plant matter, such as dead moss and dead tree bark. Nadkarni began cataloging the complex ecosystems that grow as high as 250 feet (76 m) off the ground—the height of a twenty-five-story building—in the canopies of rain forests throughout the world. She discovered that the soil found under moss in rain forest canopies is more acidic than soil on the forest floor. The acidic soil attracts certain types of insects. Many of these insects are species found only in the forest canopy. It's a unique living ecosystem.

Her discoveries validated the need for more canopy research. "Like scuba divers needing to go into the ocean's depths to understand ocean ecosystems, we [researchers] could now use that same idea [about the forest canopy]," she said.

TYPES OF FORESTS

Forests fall into three main categories: boreal, tropical, and temperate. Boreal forests are in lands in the far northern and southern parts of Earth. Coniferous species dominate these forests because they are able to withstand long cold seasons. With their evergreen needles, they can carry out photosynthesis even in winter.

Tropical forests grow in regions around the equator, an imaginary line that marks the center of Earth around a globe. This area is warm year-round. Many parts of the tropics—including large areas of Southeast Asia, central Africa, and northern South America—receive heavy rainfall. Forests that receive more than 80 inches (203 cm) of rainfall per year are called rain forests.

Temperate forests are farther to the north and south of the equator, in regions with colder weather and less rainfall. The forty-eight states of the continental United States (which does not include Hawaii and Alaska) fall into this range. Some temperate forests receive more than 80 inches (203 cm) of rain per year—so they are rain forests. A string of temperate rain forests runs along the Pacific

Ocean in North America, from southern Alaska down to Northern California. Depending on local climate, temperate forests might have to endure cold winters. The forests can consist of broadleaf trees, needleleaf trees, or a combination of both.

LAYERS OF THE FOREST

Rain forests have four levels. From top to bottom, they are the canopy, emergent layer, understory, and forest floor. Each layer receives different amounts of sunlight and water. The canopy, a layer of leafy tree crowns (tops), receives and absorbs most of the sunlight shining onto a forest. Because of all this sunshine, the canopy is also the driest and hottest area of the forest. The emergent layer, new tree growth that will eventually become the canopy, rises above the canopy. Sheltered and shaded by the canopy, large bushes, short trees, and shade-loving plants make up the understory. The forest floor is the ground floor of the forest. It is dark and moist. The leaves and other plant materials that fall to the forest floor provide food and shelter for fungi, worms, insects, and small, insect-eating animals, such as birds and frogs.

The forest floor is a dark place, but the canopy is bright with sunlight. The photosynthesis that takes place there creates fruits, flowers, and foliage, which attract diverse inhabitants. Millions of insects live in the canopy, where they eat leaves and drink nectar from flowers. The insects are in turn eaten by a variety of reptiles, birds, and mammals, which are preyed upon by other reptiles, birds, and mammals. Biologists estimate that forest canopies house more than 40 percent of the biodiversity found in land-based ecosystems and cover more than 30 percent of Earth's surface.

BACK TO THE TREETOPS

Anthropologists think that several million years ago, our prehuman ancestors, who lived in the forests of central Africa, slept in tree branches.

LAYERS OF A RAIN FOREST

emergent layer

canopy

understory

forest floor

This infographic shows the four distinct layers of a rain forest. The rain forest ecosystem varies by height. Sun-seeking plants and animals live in the highest layers. Shade-loving organisms make their homes in the understory and on the forest floor.

They were safe there from land-based predators such as cheetahs, lions, hyenas, and jackals. In the United States and elsewhere, some people in the twenty-first century build treehouse homes, where they live part-time or year-round. Some vacationers also stay in tents high up in the trees to observe wildlife there. But most modern humans live at ground level and know very little about what takes place in the forest canopy.

In the 1970s, biologists developed the single rope technique (SRT), which allowed them to explore the canopy like never before. With SRT, a researcher hangs from a rope attached to strong branches near a tree trunk. From that position, the researcher gains a close-up view of the trunk and nearby branches. But this system doesn't give access to a tree's highest leaves nor to those far from the trunk. So forest researchers modified other technologies, such as ladders, cranes, nets, towers, walkways, and even hot-air balloons, to get better access to different parts of treetops.

Imagine being a botanist studying the canopy for many hours, sometimes even overnight. You travel on catwalks tethered from tree to tree, collecting the data you'll use when you are back in your research lab. You might even sleep in a treetop hammock. Eventually you get your "tree legs." You've been above 200 feet (61 m) for so long that you think you are walking on solid ground. The canopy becomes your world. Looking out over the canopy, the notion of height disappears. It's just you, the sky, and bountiful plant and animal life.

"Our primate relatives [prehuman ancestors, as well as monkeys and apes] slept in the canopy for safety," says Nadkarni. "Once I'm all . . . secured and relaxed, I get the sense that I'm back home. In many ways, it is home. It's where we [humans] evolved from. . . . [In the canopy] there is a sense of comfort and belonging."

Meg Lowman, known as Canopy Meg, a botanist with the California Academy of Sciences, was one of the first canopy researchers. She says, "Half of my career has been devoted to inventing tools [for forest canopy research]. Most scientists have their microscope . . . already manufactured. In 1979 I was [doing graduate-degree work] in Australia and I thought, I have to get to the top of the tree because I want to study how long the leaves lived in the tropical forest." Lowman contacted a club of spelunkers,

CALIFORNIA GIANTS

The world's tallest known tree is a coast redwood (scientific name *Sequoia sempervirens*), living in Redwood National Park in California. Nicknamed Hyperion, it stood 379 feet (116 m) tall when it was measured in September 2006. Botanists estimate that Hyperion is approximately six hundred years old. This is fairly young for a coast redwood, since these trees can live for more than two thousand years. So Hyperion has lots of time to grow taller.

The largest tree in the world is a giant sequoia (*Sequoiadendron giganteum*) in Sequoia National Park in east central California. Called General Sherman, the tree is 275 feet (84 m) tall and 36 feet (11 m) in diameter at the base. General Sherman is not only large—it is also ancient. Botanists can determine a tree's age by dendrochronology, or counting the rings growing around its core, at the very center of its trunk. A new ring grows each year. It's easy to date a tree after it has been cut down: you count the rings running across its stump. Since General Sherman is alive, it can't be dated this easily. Instead, botanists have dated General Sherman by examining samples cut from its trunk combined with ring measurements from stumps of giant sequoias of similar size. Based on this work, botanists estimate General Sherman to be around 2,150 years old. That makes it only a middle-aged giant sequoia! Botanists believe that other sequoia trees are more than 3,220 years old.

or cavers. They use sturdy ropes to climb up and down the walls of caves. The club members taught her to use the same climbing techniques to explore trees. She continues, "Nowadays we have a tool kit of four or five good methods." Lowman says that the newest way to study the forest canopy is with airplanes and drones (unpiloted, remotely controlled aircraft) equipped with cameras. "To survey a forest from high up and look down is . . . exciting."

A giant sequoia tree dwarfs the log cabin standing next to it.

LUNGS OF THE EARTH

As they photosynthesize, rain forests absorb vast amounts of carbon dioxide and release great amounts of oxygen into the atmosphere. In fact, approximately 28 percent of oxygen turnover (the release of oxygen into the atmosphere during photosynthesis) takes place in rain forests.

Rain forests are home to millions of plant and animal species. Biologists don't know how many species live on Earth—and they don't know how many species live in rain forests. They use statistics and computer modeling to make their best guesses, however. In the 1980s, Terry Erwin, an entomologist at the Smithsonian Institution (a US-government-backed scientific, cultural, and educational organization in Washington, DC), calculated that Earth might be home to as many as thirty million species. Biologists think that rain forests are home to about 50 percent of these species.

NAME GAMES

All living things, including fungi, have common names, such as coast redwood or grizzly bear. Biologists also use a scientific naming system created by Swedish botanist Carolus Linnaeus in the mid-eighteenth century. The system uses Greek- and Latin-based terms to identify each organism's genus (a group of closely related organisms) and species (the specific kind within that group). For example, the scientific name for the giant sequoia tree is *Sequoiadendron giganteum*. *Sequoiadendron* is the genus name, and *giganteum* is the species name.

Genus and species are the most precise classifications for living things. But these categories fall under a larger naming umbrella consisting of eight levels: domain, kingdom, phylum, class, order, family, genus, and species. You can see the hierarchy by looking at the giant sequoia tree. It belongs to the domain Eukarya—a group that includes all plants, animals, and fungi, as well as single-celled organisms called protists. Within that category, giant sequoias belong to

- the kingdom Plantae (the plant kingdom)
- the phylum Tracheophyta (plants with xylem and phloem)
- the class Pinopsida (plants with simple leaves and male and female cones)
- the order Pinales (woody conifers with needlelike leaves)
- the family Cupressaceae (plants whose leaves and cones have specific characteristics)
- the genus *Sequoiadendron* (a group consisting of only giant sequoias and an extinct type of sequoia tree)

The species name *Sequoiadendron giganteum* is the specific designation for the giant sequoia. Each kind of living thing has its own species name, and members of the same species can mate with one another to reproduce.

But rain forests and the species that call them home are in danger. Every day, humans destroy more than 80,000 acres (32,000 ha) of tropical rain forest and significantly degrade another 80,000 acres on top of that. Humans inflict this damage when they cut down trees to make wood products, such as paper and furniture; build homes and other structures in previously forested areas; and clear forests to establish farms, mines, and ranches.

When rain forests are destroyed or degraded, the animals and plants that live there often die because they lose the food and shelter that forests provide them. As buildings, roads, and other human-made structures fill up the forest ecosystem, animal habitats (home territories) become fragmented. Male and female animals have to cross roads and travel through human-occupied areas to find one another for mating. As this becomes increasingly difficult and dangerous, animal mating declines, fewer babies are born, and population numbers start to dwindle.

Because of deforestation, pollution, climate change, and other human activities, Earth's plant and animal species are going extinct (or dying out) in record numbers. No one knows exactly how many species are dying out because no one knows exactly how many plant and animal species live on Earth. But the Switzerland-based International Union for Conservation of Nature (IUCN) believes that 13 percent of birds, 26 percent of mammals, and 42 percent of amphibians are threatened with extinction.

Loss of forests and their rich biodiversity is a critical issue for the health of Earth. Paul Ehrlich, president of the Center for Conservation Biology and Bing Professor of Population Studies at Stanford University in California, compares biodiversity to the mechanical parts of an airplane. If an airplane mechanic continued to remove nuts and bolts from a plane, the plane would not fly and would fall apart. Similarly, if trees and other plants disappear, the forest ecosystem will fall apart. Forest plants and animals will die. So to preserve the health of Earth and its living things, it is crucial to protect forests.

CHAPTER 5

LISTENING TO FORESTS

IT'S EXCITING TO USE THIS DATA TO
FIND ANSWERS THAT ARE MEANINGFUL
TO PEOPLE'S LIVES AND THE EARTH.
WITH REMOTE SENSING, WE HAVE A NEW
LEVEL OF DETAIL THAT WE DIDN'T HAVE
BEFORE ABOUT FORESTS.

—Geographer Paulo Arevalo Orduz

The Amazon rain forest, which surrounds the Amazon River in Brazil, Peru, Colombia, Bolivia, Venezuela, Suriname, Guyana, and French Guiana in South America, is Earth's largest rain forest. It is home to approximately 10 percent of the known species of plants and animals in the world. Like all forests, the Amazon releases oxygen and absorbs carbon dioxide in the process of photosynthesis.

Until the mid-twentieth century, local farmers were usually the only people cutting down trees in the Amazon. They did so to clear farmland to grow crops for their families. This logging did not significantly harm the forest because it took place on a very small scale. But in the late twentieth century, humans cut or burned down large

The Amazon rain forest is home to millions of plants and animals, like this Brazilian tanager. When humans destroy rain forests, they also destroy plant and animal habitat.

portions of the Amazon to make room for large-scale farms, ranches, industrial buildings, roads, and other human-made structures. Between 1978 and 2018, more than 290,000 square miles (750,000 sq. km) of Amazon rain forest were destroyed.

This destruction harmed plants and animals that made their homes in the rain forest. It also increased the effects of climate change. A mature forest absorbs hundreds of tons of carbon dioxide over many centuries. When a forest is destroyed, either by fire or cutting, much of that carbon dioxide is released into the atmosphere. More carbon dioxide in the air traps more heat from the sun, and climate change grows more extreme. In fact, deforestation and forest degradation account for approximately 10 to 15 percent of all carbon dioxide emissions on Earth. That's more carbon dioxide than comes from all the cars and other fossil-fuel-burning vehicles on the planet.

If deforestation plays such a big role in climate change, why not just plant new forests to fight climate change? The answer is that large, old trees collect and store more carbon dioxide than smaller, younger trees, so a young forest cannot take in as much carbon dioxide as an old forest. In fact, it can take one hundred years for a replanted forest to absorb as much carbon dioxide as the original forest did before it was cut. So, in the short term, replanting forests does not significantly offset the effects of climate change.

In addition, young, replanted forests are usually not as biodiverse as old, natural forests. Because they are less diverse, they are more easily wiped out by diseases and insects. In large, old forests with a variety of tree species, certain types of trees will survive an infestation, even if many other species die. So the forest itself will live on—and will continue to absorb carbon dioxide.

SEEING REDD+

The urgent need to reduce carbon dioxide emissions to combat climate change has led to numerous international efforts to protect existing forests. One of these programs is Reducing Emissions from Deforestation and Forest Degradation (REDD+). The United Nations, an international humanitarian and peacekeeping organization, developed this program in 2008. REDD+ encourages nations to protect their forests by making payments to those that say no to forest destruction and degradation.

To receive payment from REDD+, a nation must show that it has protected its forests and increased its acreage of forest land. In doing so, the nation is increasing the amount of carbon stored there. Measuring the amount of forested lands can be done in several ways. On-site measurement (physically measuring and mapping forests at ground level) is one method. But it's much easier to take measurements from the air, using a method called remote sensing. Remote sensing involves collecting information about objects on Earth without making physical contact with them. The most common remote-sensing tools are cameras and sensors on satellites and aircraft. The cameras take images. The sensors measure light and other types of energy in forests and measure atmospheric substances such as carbon dioxide. By taking the measurements over a period of time, scientists can track changes to follow degradation or improvement.

STUDENTS AND TECHNOLOGY TO THE RESCUE

Countries that are attempting to regrow, protect, and measure forest lands with REDD+ and other programs need the help of trained scientists. Paulo Arevalo Orduz, a PhD student studying geography at Boston University in Massachusetts, is one such expert. He and his colleagues help the South American nation of Colombia measure its forest-covered lands. They use satellite images, maps provided by the National Aeronautics and Space Administration (NASA, a US government agency), and other remote-sensing technology to measure forests and their carbon dioxide emissions. "We calculate the carbon emissions for an area, such as the Colombia Amazon, by understanding how the land has changed over time," Arevalo Orduz says. He also looks at new trees growing in previously cut forests and attempts to measure that growth.

> "NOT ONLY CAN WE MAP FOREST LOSS, WE CAN MAP HOW THE LAND IS USED AFTER THE FOREST IS GONE AND WHETHER THE FOREST GROWS BACK."
>
> —Paulo Arevalo Orduz

LISTENING TO FORESTS

SCIENTIST PROFILE: PAULO AREVALO ORDUZ

Paulo Arevalo Orduz grew up in Bogotá, the capital of Colombia. The city is home to more than eight million people. As a child, Arevalo Orduz enjoyed reading books and solving problems, especially problems that required using a map. In a college geography course in Colombia, he learned that satellites continuously collect information about the entire planet. He was hooked. He wanted to explore all the possibilities of satellite technology, including the remote-sensing data they provide.

In September 2014, Arevalo Orduz started pursuing a doctorate in geography at Boston University. When he began the program, he didn't have the advanced computer-coding skills he needed to solve complex remote-sensing problems. He could code, but not as well as his fellow students. To learn what he needed, Arevalo Orduz read a lot, used online resources, and asked questions of students who already had coding skills.

Arevalo Orduz struggled with transitioning to a new country and a new school. He considered dropping out of college. Then cold, snowy winter came to Boston, and he wanted to leave even more. He missed his warm, tropical home of Bogotá. But his professors and fellow students encouraged him to keep learning and working hard. He was inspired by all the smart, supportive people in his field. They believed in him, and he chose to stay. After graduation he plans to work for an organization that uses remote-sensing data to address global problems, including climate change.

Usually, it takes more than ten years to regrow a forest. But in some places, regrowth is very fast—four to five years. To see the growth, Arevalo Orduz uses statistics, mathematics, and computer programs to "look for things that look different."

The goal for his work is to provide a method—similar to a recipe or set of instructions—for countries to use to monitor their forests and carbon dioxide emissions. Arevalo Orduz and his colleagues are working closely with Colombia's national environmental agency to develop this recipe. Part of the recipe will involve training researchers in Colombia and elsewhere to do their own remote sensing.

"It's exciting to use this data to find answers that are meaningful to people's lives and the earth," says Arevalo Orduz. "With remote sensing, we have a new level of detail that we didn't have before about forests. Remote-sensing technologies make it possible to investigate deforestation and forest degradation in new ways. For example, not only can we map forest loss, we can map how the land is used after the forest is gone and whether the forest grows back. Other technologies . . . allow us to map three-dimensional structures of the forest."

One of these other technologies is lidar—light detection and ranging—a remote-sensing method used to measure forests and other Earth features. This satellite-based system uses pulses of light to create three-dimensional maps of forests, rock formations, deserts, rivers, and other geographic features. NASA makes its lidar technology available to researchers. Arevalo Orduz says, "These [technologies] improve our understanding of forest degradation and our estimates of carbon . . . emissions. With these new technologies come new discoveries and new questions."

HOW DO WE SAVE OUR FORESTS?

Researchers have identified the factors, across countries, that lead to either more or less deforestation. Governments, scientific organizations, and ordinary citizens can be mindful of these factors. They can

LANDSAT

NASA and the US Geological Survey (USGS) operate a satellite called Landsat (Land Remote-Sensing Satellite). Launched in 1972 and replaced every few years, Landsat orbits Earth and photographs the entire surface of the planet. In 2008 the USGS made the data from Landsat available and free to the public on its website. Countries that participate in REDD+ can use this satellite data to monitor their forests. They can also use the data to compare Landsat photographs of the same forest taken at different times to see if it has grown or shrunk. Brazil was one of the first countries to use Landsat technology. Other nations, including China, Australia, and India, use Landsat data as well as data from their own satellites to track forest coverage and loss. Additional satellite images are available from the Jet Propulsion Laboratory, NASA's California-based center for robotic exploration of the solar system. Images are also available from the Woods Hole Research Center, a scientific organization in Massachusetts that focuses on climate change and solutions.

encourage practices and efforts that lead to less deforestation and discourage those that lead to more deforestation.

Programs such as REDD+, which pay nations to protect forests, make citizens aware of the value of forests while providing an incentive to protect them. Strict local and federal laws can also protect forests, by making it a crime to remove large numbers of trees in certain areas, for instance. Governments can designate forests as protected areas, where logging, building, and other human activities are not allowed. In the United States, national parks are examples of protected land, although in the twenty-first century, climate change threatens these parks and many powerful industries want to open them up to logging, mining, and oil drilling.

All over the world, forests are being cut or burned down so the land can be used for planting crops and raising livestock on a massive scale. In many places where tropical forests once thrived, farmers instead grow soybeans, coffee, corn, cacao beans, and sugarcane, and ranchers raise beef cattle. Some paper companies cut down forests to make paper, only to replant the land with fast-growing trees that are soon cut to make more paper. The more people demand forest products, the more forests will be cut down. The solutions are complex. One issue is that Earth's growing population—which tops seven billion—puts pressure on our shared natural resources, including forests. A greater number of people means the need for more food, more homes, and more roads, all of which threaten wooded lands.

This area where cattle graze in Brazil was formerly covered by rain forest. A single Brazil nut tree and a few other rain forest plants are all that remain.

LISTENING TO FORESTS

MEATLESS MONDAY

Producing meat eats up vast amounts of precious resources, such as water and land. In Brazil and elsewhere, thousands of acres of rain forest have been cleared to raise livestock. And when forests are cleared to build ranches, fewer trees are left to absorb carbon dioxide from the atmosphere—so climate change gains speed.

One solution? Eat less meat! The organization Meatless Monday, based in Baltimore, Maryland, educates people on the health and environmental benefits of giving up meat for just one day per week. Launched with the Johns Hopkins Bloomberg School of Public Health in 2003, Meatless Monday is active in more than forty countries. Restaurants, schools, hospitals, and other institutions have all signed on to skip serving meat on Mondays. By joining the movement, you can make a difference.

The way we eat also puts a strain on forests and other resources. Many experts recommend relying less on a meat-based diet in favor of plant-based eating. A plant-heavy diet can have positive health effects. And if enough people around the world eat less meat, livestock producers might raise fewer animals and cut down fewer forests to provide grazing lands. Consumers can also use less paper to reduce the number of trees cut to make paper products. On a large scale, choices like these can make a difference.

ALTERNATIVES TO CLEAR-CUT LOGGING

As the breakfast list of tree-based products showed, people use a lot of wood from trees. Instead of clear-cutting forests to get that wood, which involves removing all the trees from a forest, foresters can remove trees in ways that preserve the forest. And they can plant new trees in ways that work with natural forest ecosystems.

For example, in a branch of forestry called silviculture (*silvi* means "forest" or "wood" in Latin), foresters extract trees one at a time or in small clearings. New saplings naturally spring up between the cut trees, taking advantage of the new shafts of sunlight reaching through to the forest floor. Used in northern Europe for hundreds of years, silviculture works with nature rather than against it. But it is more labor intensive and time consuming than clear-cutting. Silviculture requires people to select and carefully remove only a few trees. Large-scale logging operations don't work this way. Instead, they use power saws and big machinery to remove many trees in a short time and with fewer people required to do the work.

DIVERSE FORESTS, WITH TREES OF A VARIETY OF AGES AND SPECIES, ARE BETTER ABLE TO WEATHER DISEASE, INSECT INFESTATIONS, AND OTHER THREATS THAN ARE FORESTS WITH TREES OF ALL ONE SPECIES AND SIMILAR AGES.

Foresters can also use techniques called coppicing and pollarding to produce new trees quickly. Many broadleaf trees, such as hazelnut, chestnut, oak, and ash trees, do not die when they are cut down. Instead, new shoots grow from buds at the bases of their cut trunks. Because the trunks are connected to well-developed root systems, the saplings grow to adulthood very rapidly. They can be harvested every ten years. Coppicing involves cutting down young trees right at the base and allowing new trees to grow from the cut stumps.

SISTER DOROTHY STANG

Dorothy Stang (1931–2005), a Catholic nun from Ohio, worked in the Brazilian state of Para for nearly forty years. Her work involved advocating for poor rural people and trying to protect rain forests from destruction. Many cattle ranchers in the area wanted to cut down forests so they could raise more cattle on the cleared land. More cattle meant more money for the ranchers. They didn't like it when Stang and others spoke out against deforestation.

On February 12, 2005, Stang was on her way to a meeting with a local farmer to discuss ways to protect the forest. She was approached by two armed men who worked for a livestock business in Para. They had been hired to kill her so she could no longer speak out against deforestation. One of the men did so with shots to her abdomen, back, and head.

News of Stang's death brought worldwide public outrage and put pressure on Brazil's government to act. The shooter and his accomplices were arrested, convicted, and sent to prison. The killing and associated public outrage awakened the Brazilian government to the violence associated with deforestation and inspired its determination to prevent deforestation.

American nun Dorothy Stang worked to protect Brazilian rain forests from destruction. Her work angered Brazilian ranchers, and one of them had her killed in 2005.

Pollarding involves cutting young trees about 6 to 9 feet (2 to 3 m) off the ground. New trees grow from the top of the cut trunk, creating an interesting-looking tree with trees growing on top of it. Traditionally, foresters used coppicing and pollarding to obtain wood without destroying a forest. The same techniques are used in modern times for the same reason.

Instead of planting a single species of tree to replace a destroyed forest, some foresters use approaches that mimic nature. For example, they plant trees in mixed-age and mixed-species stands, producing conditions similar to those of natural forests. Diverse forests, with trees of a variety of ages and species, are better able to weather disease, insect infestations, and other threats than are forests with trees of all one species and similar ages.

LESSONS FROM BRAZIL

The Brazilian Amazon once had the highest rate of deforestation in the world. Between 1978 and 2017, people destroyed more than 290,000 square miles (750,000 sq. km) of rain forest in the Amazon—an area roughly the size of the state of Texas—and 79 percent of that destruction took place in Brazil. But in 2004, the people of Brazil—at the federal, state, and local levels—took action. Brazil reduced its rate of deforestation by 80 percent in six years. How did Brazil do it?

First, the Brazilian government outlawed logging in certain areas. But the Brazilian rain forest is immense, and law enforcement agents couldn't be everywhere at once to detect illegal logging. Technology came to the rescue. In May 2004, the Brazilian National Institute for Space Research launched the Real-Time System for Detection of Deforestation program. This satellite-based system photographs Earth from space, detects forest clearings in the Brazilian Amazon, and sends biweekly alerts to federal and state law enforcement agencies. Law enforcement agents use this information to identify areas where forests are being cleared illegally. Agents then make arrests, which can

LISTENING TO FORESTS

lead to punishment for companies or individuals responsible for the deforestation, and they put up barriers to block access to the affected forest. The program has played a key part in helping Brazil reduce its Amazon deforestation.

Brazil also established new protected areas and enforced protection of existing protected areas. An example is the Xingu Extractive Reserve, known locally as Xingu Resex, in the state of Para. The Brazilian government established the 750,000-acre (303,000 ha) park in 2008. It is home to an indigenous group named the Xingu. Their ancestors have lived in this territory for thousands of years. Mining, logging, and professional hunting are prohibited in the park. So Xingu Resex is much like a US national park—except that people are allowed to make their homes there year-round.

INDIGENOUS PEOPLES WHO MAKE THEIR HOMES IN THE FOREST KNOW HOW TO LISTEN TO THE TREES. THEY LIVE IN HARMONY WITH THE FOREST ECOSYSTEM.

Brazil also minimized road construction through rain forests and increased law enforcement on existing roads through forests. Loggers had used these roads to access forests for illegal logging. With fewer roads and increased law enforcement, illegal loggers have a harder time carrying out their operations.

Brazil has also worked to protect its forests from clear-cutting for farmland. This is a challenging task, since Brazilian-raised beef, soybeans, palm oil, paper, and timber are sold around the world and have earned Brazil a lot of money. But Brazil is a large nation. It is almost as big as the United States. It has enough land to raise food crops and livestock without cutting down additional rain forests. The Brazilian government has used legislation and land management to protect its remaining rain forests. It has limited the clearing of land for agriculture and replanted some forests that were cleared for agriculture in the past.

Finally, Brazil has encouraged citizens living along rivers in the Amazon not to turn their forests into farmland. For example, Brazil's Bolsa Floresta program, led by the Amazonas Sustainable Foundation, provides rural families with a small payment and benefits such as education and health care in exchange for promising not to cut or burn down forests to clear land for farming. The program helps participants generate income in other ways, through eco-friendly businesses such as ecotourism, fish farming, and honey production.

NEXT STEPS

> TREES ARE SANCTUARIES. WHOEVER KNOWS HOW TO SPEAK TO THEM, WHOEVER KNOWS HOW TO LISTEN TO THEM, CAN LEARN THE TRUTH.
> —German author Hermann Hesse, *Wandering*, 1920

Indigenous peoples who make their homes in the forest, such as the Mbuti Pygmies in Africa and the Xingu in the Amazon, know how to listen to the trees. They live in harmony with the forest ecosystem. But their homes and their traditional ways of life are threatened by deforestation, climate change, and pollution. They understand the dire implications of losing Earth's forests.

URBAN FORESTS

People who live in cities might think of forests as something remote and not integral to their lives. But that's far from the truth. City dwellers rely on forests for food, medicine, and other products, as well

This tree-lined walkway in a park in Charleston, South Carolina, provides a shady haven for city residents and visitors.

as for their mental health. Urban ecologists are scientists who study how plants and animals in a city relate to one another and to their surroundings. Urban foresters are biologists who plant and care for trees in cities. These specialists encourage cities to plant trees. Diane Pataki, a professor of biology at the University of Utah in Salt Lake City, says, "There should be trees everywhere [in cities] because the benefits outweigh the costs. We need to know a lot more [about] how trees help people . . . so we can plant the right trees for the right spaces and communities."

Vincent Callebaut calls himself an archibiotect. He coined the term—a combination of *architect* and *biotech*—to describe his approach to building. Based in Paris, France, Callebaut designs buildings that produce their own power, house thousands of plants to take carbon dioxide from the air, and contain greenhouses for producing food.

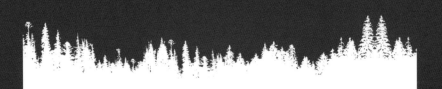

FORESTS ON THE MOVE

With climate change and warming temperatures on Earth, plants and animals are reacting. Many animal species have responded to higher temperatures by moving north and to higher elevations, where temperatures are cooler. Plants and even whole forests have also begun to move.

How does a forest move? Imagine a North American forest of Douglas fir trees, which prefer cold weather. As Earth's temperatures rise, new saplings might grow in abundance on the northern edge of the forest, where temperatures are cooler. Meanwhile, on the southern edge of the forest, where temperatures are higher, older trees will die and fewer new saplings will grow. Over time, as more trees grow to the north and the southern trees die out, the entire forest literally shifts its position.

Songlin Fei, a professor of forestry at Purdue University in Indiana, has tracked the movement of eighty-six tree species across the eastern United States over three decades. His study found that many trees are moving north to colder climates. But it also found that more trees are moving west than north.

Fei explains that due to climate change, the western part of his study area is receiving more rain than the eastern part. "Different species are responding to climate change differently," he says. "Most of the broad-leaf species—deciduous trees—are following moisture moving westward. The evergreen trees—the needle species—are primarily moving northward [to find cooler weather]." Other issues, such as pests, disease, and wildfire, might also be pushing forests toward the west.

If evergreen trees are moving north and deciduous trees are moving west, how will this affect tree communities in forests? Think about the paper birch and Douglas fir, which share resources to help each other survive. If they no longer live in the same forest, what happens to them? Researchers such as Fei intend to find out.

His projects include Tao Zhu Yin Yuan Tower in Taipei, Taiwan, completed in 2018. The twenty-one-story apartment complex contains twenty-three thousand trees and plants, designed to absorb 130 tons (118 t) of carbon dioxide each year.

Many organizations are dedicated to planting trees in urban settings. Afforestt in Bangalore, India, and Natural Urban Forests in Seattle, Washington, collaborate on growing "microforests"—tiny forests—in cities. Microforests can cover as little as 1,000 square feet (93 sq. m)—about the size of a one-bedroom apartment—and can have as few as three hundred trees. Because they are designed to be self-sustaining ecosystems, these forests grow to maturity in one to two years—ten times faster than forests planted by logging and paper companies. They are also thirty times denser and one hundred times more biodiverse than conventionally grown forests. When establishing microforests, foresters choose trees and shrubs that are native to the area and that naturally communicate with and help one another through airborne chemicals and mycorrhizal networks. Indian engineer Shubhendu Sharma, who founded Afforestt in 2011, planted his first microforest in his own backyard. Since then, Afforestt and Natural Urban Forests have established more than one hundred microforests worldwide—containing more than four hundred thousand trees—in vacant lots, backyards, schoolyards, and even on the grounds of factories.

HELPING TREES HELP US

Wherever you live, you can help forests and trees. Many organizations sponsor tree-planting projects around the United States and around the world. To find out about projects where you live, type the name of your city or state and the keywords "tree planting" and "volunteering" into a search engine and see what shows up. You don't need to plant a whole microforest to help Earth. You can start by planting just one tree in your own backyard or neighborhood.

WANGARI MAATHAI

What started as a quest for food, water, and firewood became a victory for trees and people. In the 1970s, women in rural Kenya noted that the streams where they collected drinking water were drying up, that their food crops were vulnerable to drought and disease, and that they had to walk farther and farther to gather firewood for heating and cooking. Wangari Maathai (*right*), a Kenyan university professor and environmentalist, suggested that the women plant trees. She knew that the new trees would be part of the water cycle. They would take up water through their roots, store it in their trunks, and release it into the air via their leaves. The process would create more rain, which would nourish more trees. Fallen leaves, dead bark, and other matter from the trees would enrich the soil.

Maathai founded the nonprofit Green Belt Movement in 1977. The group started in Kenya and spread to other African nations. Since Maathai founded the movement, participants have planted more than fifty-one million trees. In addition to tree planting, the Green Belt Movement trains women in forestry, farming, beekeeping, and other eco-friendly income-generating activities. The organization also protests policies and activities that hurt African women, children, the environment, and communities.

In 2004 Maathai received the Nobel Peace Prize for her contributions to economic development, democracy, and peace. In a film about Wangari Maathai and the Green Belt Movement called *Taking Root*, she said, "It is the people who must save the environment. It is the people who must make their leaders change. And we cannot be intimidated. So we must stand up for what we believe in."

Each year Americans of all ages celebrate Arbor Day on the last Friday in April. It is a holiday dedicated to planting trees.

You can help trees in many other ways too. For one thing, make sure that the forest-derived products you buy are made from 100 percent recycled materials. For example, when you buy paper for your computer printer, choose recycled paper. When people use recycled paper, fewer trees are cut down to make paper from scratch.

Also consider your food choices. Choosing to eat vegetarian meals and reducing your meat consumption can help save forests. That's because massive areas of tropical forest have been cut down to make room for cattle ranches. This destruction will not stop if people continue to consume large amounts of beef. But if consumers eat less beef, fewer forests will be cleared for ranching.

Buy from companies that have forest-friendly policies. Many popular foods, such as chocolate, coconut, coffee, vanilla, cinnamon, and pepper, come from rain forests around the world. Growers can harvest these products responsibly—without damaging the trees and plants that supply them and without damaging the rain forest ecosystem—or they can harvest them irresponsibly.

The Forest Stewardship Council label on this garden tool indicates that the wood in the tool was grown and harvested using forest-friendly methods.

Consider palm oil, made from the fruit of the oil palm tree. Palm oil is found in thousands of processed food and household items—everything from ice cream to margarine to soap to cosmetics. On the Indonesian island of Sumatra in Southeast Asia, agricultural companies have cut down millions of acres of rain forest to create oil palm plantations. The deforestation has destroyed the homes of Sumatran orangutans, elephants, tigers, and rhinoceroses—threatening them with extinction. But it's possible to produce palm oil without cutting down rain forests. Growers simply need to plant oil palms on existing farmland or land that has previously been cleared for other uses. In Sumatra an organization of growers called the Palm Oil Innovation Group is doing just that. Its members have committed themselves to raising oil palms without cutting down any more rain forests.

You can support forest-friendly organizations by buying their products. Look for labels from the Rainforest Alliance, the Forest Stewardship Council, the Roundtable on Sustainable Palm Oil, and other groups that work to preserve forests. These labels let you know that a grower or manufacturer has used forest-friendly methods and ingredients to make its products. Let manufacturers know you care about these issues. Send an email or other communication to congratulate them if they protect forests, and let them know your concerns if they don't. If companies realize their customers care, they will too.

Share what you have learned about helping forests with your friends, family, and community so they can help too. Explore science careers that help trees and forests. But perhaps most important, get outside! Take a hike with friends and family among the trees or in the forest. Spend time forest bathing so you can relax and listen to the forest talk.

GLOSSARY

biodiversity: the number of different plant and animal species in a place or region. Biodiversity is essential to the health of an ecosystem because plants and animals rely on one another for food, pollination, distribution of seeds, and other biological processes. In addition, in forests with many different tree species, some species will survive an infestation of disease or insects, even if other species die. So biodiversity keeps the forest from being destroyed completely.

broadleaf trees: trees with flat, wide leaves with veins running through them. Their seeds grow inside fruits. In temperate (mild) climates, most broadleaf trees lose their leaves in fall and winter. They grow new leaves in spring.

canopy: the uppermost layer of a forest, formed by the branches and leaves of the tallest trees. The canopy receives and absorbs most of the sunlight reaching a forest.

carbon cycle: the series of natural and industrial processes by which carbon travels through the environment. In the natural carbon cycle, carbon moves through the air, water, soil, plants, and animals in an endless loop. By burning fossil fuels, people have put extra carbon into the cycle.

carbon dioxide: a colorless and odorless greenhouse gas vital to life on Earth. All green plants use carbon dioxide to make food. Carbon dioxide traps heat from the sun near Earth, and extra carbon dioxide in the atmosphere, caused by the burning of fossil fuels, has led to rising temperatures and climate change.

climate change: in the modern era, the warming of Earth's atmosphere caused by the burning of fossil fuels. The release of heat-trapping carbon dioxide into the atmosphere has altered Earth's climate and led to more extreme weather, including droughts, floods, and ferocious storms.

conifer: a type of tree or shrub that bears its seeds in cones. Most conifers are evergreen and have small, needlelike leaves.

deciduous tree: a tree that loses its leaves in fall and grows new ones in spring. Most broadleaf trees are deciduous.

deforestation: the loss of a forest for any reason. Deforestation often occurs when people cut or burn down trees to make room for farms, ranches, homes, roads, and industry.

dendrochronology: the science of counting growth rings in living trees and old wood to determine the age of trees. Dendrochronology is also used to date events that occurred during the lifetimes of the trees being studied.

ecosystem: an ecological community consisting of interdependent biological and physical entities. The biological members of an ecosystem are the plants and animals that live there. The physical members are elements such as air, soil, water, and weather. Members of an ecosystem interact with and depend on one another.

epiphyte: a plant that grows on another plant but makes its own food. Epiphytes are not parasites. They take most of the moisture and nutrients they need directly from the air and from dead plant matter that accumulates around their roots. Their roots are not attached to the soil. Some mosses, orchids, and ferns are epiphytes.

extinct: having no living members. A species becomes extinct when the last individual of that species dies.

forest: a large area of land covered with trees. A forest also includes the smaller plants that live there, such as shrubs, mosses, and flowers. It includes the birds, insects, and other animals that make their homes there as well.

forest degradation: harm to or partial destruction of the forest ecosystem. Many human activities lead to forest degradation. For instance, polluting air and water can harm plants and animals and degrade a forest.

forest ecology: the scientific study of how living organisms relate to one another and to their surroundings in a forest

forestry: the science or practice of planting, managing, and caring for forests

fungus: an organism that obtains food by absorbing it from other living things or from dead plant and animal matter. Examples of fungi are mildews, molds, and mushrooms.

humus: nutrient-rich soil resulting from the decomposition of plant or animal matter

indigenous people: a group whose ancestors were the original human inhabitants of a specific location or region. For instance, American Indians are indigenous peoples of the Americas.

light detection and ranging (lidar): a satellite-based system that uses pulses of light to create three-dimensional maps of forests, rock formations, deserts, rivers, and other geographic features on Earth

mycorrhizal fungus: a fungus that forms symbiotic relationships with the roots of trees or other plants. In this relationship, the roots give carbon from the plant to the fungi, and the fungi supply water and minerals from the soil to the roots.

needleleaf tree: a tree with needlelike leaves. Most needleleaf trees keep their leaves all year-round, so they are "ever green," which is why they are also called evergreens. Needleleaf trees are called coniferous trees because their seeds grow inside cones.

oxygen turnover: the release of oxygen into the atmosphere during photosynthesis. Rain forests are responsible for approximately 28 percent of the oxygen turnover on Earth.

parasite: a living thing that feeds off another living thing. Some fungi are parasites.

photosynthesis: the process by which green plants combine sunlight, carbon dioxide, and water to make food

rain forest: a forest growing in a region of abundant rainfall (at least 80 inches [203 cm] per year). Most rain forests grow in tropical areas with year-round warm weather.

silviculture: the science of managing forests in a way that protects the ecosystem. When harvesting trees from forests, silviculturists extract them one at a time from small clearings. New saplings then grow between the cut trees.

symbiotic relationship: a relationship that is beneficial to all the groups involved. For example, because they give one another water, minerals, and carbon, trees and mycorrhizal fungi have a symbiotic relationship.

transpiration: the passage of water from a living thing, such as a tree leaf, into the atmosphere

water cycle: the ongoing movement of Earth's water from the oceans to the air to the land and back to the oceans. Trees take part in the water cycle by taking up water through their roots and releasing it into the atmosphere through their leaves.

SELECTED BIBLIOGRAPHY

Anderson, Maximo. "Brazil's 'River People' Join Forces with Indigenous Communities, Offer Alternative to Deforestation." Mongabay, February 10, 2017. https://news.mongabay.com/2017/02/brazils-river-people-join-forces-with -indigenous-communities-offer-alternative-to-deforestation.

Biba, Erin. "Awesome Jobs: Meet Meg Lowman, Tree Canopy Biologist." Adam Savage's Tested, September 9, 2014. http://www.tested.com/science/464599 -awesome-jobs-meet-meg-lowman-tree-canopy-biologist/.

Butler, Rhett. "Calculating Deforestation Figures for the Amazon." Mongabay, January 26, 2017. https://rainforests.mongabay.com/amazon/deforestation _calculations.html.

Ennos, R. *Trees: A Complete Guide to Their Biology and Structure.* Ithaca, NY: Cornell University Press, 2016.

Groetzinger, Kate. "World Health Organization: People in 80% of Reporting Cities Are Breathing Harmful Air." Quartz, May 13, 2016. https://qz.com/682942 /who-report-people-in-80-of-reporting-cities-are-breathing-harmful-air/.

Hausfather, Zeke. "Analysis: Global CO2 Emissions Set to Rise 2% in 2017 after Three-Year Plateau." Carbon Brief, December 13, 2017. https://www.carbonbrief .org/analysis-global-co2-emissions-set-to-rise-2-percent-in-2017-following-three -year-plateau.

Konkel, Lindsey. "Trees, Science, and the Goodness of Green Space." Environmental Health News, April 11, 2017. https://www.ehn.org/trees_science_and_the _goodness_of_green_space-2497193710.html.

Kuo, Ming. "How Might Contact with Nature Promote Human Health? Promising Mechanisms and a Possible Central Pathway." *Frontiers in Psychology*, August 25, 2015. https://doi.org/10.3389/fpsyg.2015.01093.

Lowman, Margaret D., E. Burgess, and J. Burgess. *It's a Jungle Up There: More Tales from the Treetops.* New Haven, CT: Yale University Press, 2006.

Nadkarni, Nalini. *Between Earth and Sky: Our Intimate Connections to Trees.* Berkeley: University of California Press, 2009.

Noë, Alva. "A Web of Trees and Their 'Hidden' Lives." *National Public Radio*, September 23, 2016. https://www.npr.org/sections/13.7/2016/09/23/494989594 /a-web-of-trees-and-their-hidden-lives.

Preston, R. *Wild Trees: A Story of Passion and Daring.* New York: Random House, 2008.

Seymour, F., and J. Busch. *Why Forests? Why Now?* Washington, DC: Center for Global Development, 2016.

Watts, Jonathan. "Alarm as Study Reveals World's Tropical Forests Are Huge Carbon Emission Source." *Guardian* (US ed.), September 28, 2017. https://www .theguardian.com/environment/2017/sep/28/alarm-as-study-reveals-worlds -tropical-forests-are-huge-carbon-emission-source.

Wohlleben, Peter. *The Hidden Life of Trees: What They Feel, How They Communicate; Discoveries from a Secret World*. Vancouver, BC: Greystone Books, 2016.

FURTHER INFORMATION

BOOKS

Blevins, Wiley. *Ninja Plants: Survival and Adaptation in the Plant World*. Minneapolis: Twenty-First Century Books, 2017.

Chazdon, Robin. *Second Growth: The Promise of Tropical Forest Generation in an Age of Deforestation*. Chicago: University of Chicago Press, 2014.

Florence, Namulundah. *Wangari Maathai: Visionary, Environmental Leader, Political Activist*. Herndon, VA: Lantern Books, 2014.

Heos, Bridget. *It's Getting Hot in Here: The Past, Present, and Future of Climate Change*. Boston: HMH Books for Young Readers, 2016.

Hughes, Meredith Sayles. *Plants vs. Meats: The Health, History, and Ethics of What We Eat*. Minneapolis: Twenty-First Century Books, 2016.

Juniper, Tony. *Rainforest: Dispatches from Earth's Most Vital Frontlines*. London: Profile Books, 2018.

Kallen, Stuart A. *Trashing the Planet: Examining Our Global Garbage Glut*. Minneapolis: Twenty-First Century Books, 2017.

Llewellyn, Robert, and Joan Maloof. *The Living Forest: A Visual Journey into the Heart of the Woods*. Portland, OR: Timber, 2017.

McGraw, Sally. *Living Simply: A Teen Guide to Minimalism*. Minneapolis: Twenty-First Century Books, 2019.

Miyazaki, Yoshifumi. *Shinrin Yoku: The Japanese Art of Forest Bathing*. Portland, OR: Timber, 2018.

Phillips, Michael. *Mycorrhizal Planet: How Symbiotic Fungi Work with Roots to Support Plant Health and Build Soil Fertility*. White River Junction, VT: Chelsea Green, 2017.

Rutkow, Eric. *American Canopy: Trees, Forests, and the Making of a Nation*. New York: Scribner, 2013.

WEBSITES

Afforestt
> https://www.afforestt.com
> Founded in 2011, India-based Afforestt creates "backyard forests" in urban areas and teaches its techniques to those who want to grow their own tiny forests.

Arbor Day Foundation
> https://www.arborday.org
> The Arbor Day Foundation is dedicated to replanting damaged forests, planting trees in urban areas, and planting trees after natural disasters. The group's name comes from Arbor Day, a holiday dedicated to trees. It takes place on the last Friday in April in the United States and on different days in other countries.

CoRenewal
> http://www.amazonmycorenewal.org
> Formerly known as the Amazon MycoRenewal Project, CoRenewal is using petroleum-eating fungi to clean up abandoned oil pits in Ecuador. It hopes to use the same technology to clean up other contaminated sites.

International Canopy Network
> http://internationalcanopynetwork.org
> Founded by Nalini Nadkarni, who in 1981 discovered tree roots growing high in the forest canopy, ICAN is dedicated to studying the canopy and its unique lifeforms.

One Tree Planted
> https://onetreeplanted.org
> Vermont-based One Tree Planted sponsors tree-planting projects around the world. For funding, it relies on donations, and each dollar the organization receives pays for the planting of one tree.

Rainforest Foundation
> http://www.rainforestfoundation.org
> Founded by British musician Sting and Trudie Styler, the Rainforest Foundation works to fight deforestation in the Amazon and also to protect the rights of indigenous communities who call the rain forest home.

VIDEOS

Heroes of the High Frontier. YouTube video, 53:35. Posted by "Qemetiel 218," October 10, 2017. https://www.youtube.com/watch?v=U36xKZ96twk. Posted on YouTube, this National Geographic film follows forest canopy researchers high into the treetops.

"How Trees Talk to Each Other." TED Talks, 18:20. June 2016. https://www.ted .com/talks/suzanne_simard_how_trees_talk_to_each_other/up-next. In this TED Talk, British Columbia forester Suzanne Simard explains her groundbreaking 1997 experiment in which she discovered that paper birch and Douglas fir trees in a forest were sharing carbon through an underground fungal network.

Intelligent Trees. DVD and streaming video. Pattensen, Germany: Dorcon Film, 2016, https://www.intelligent-trees.com. Featuring forester Peter Wohlleben, author of *The Hidden Life of Trees*, and University of British Columbia professor Suzanne Simard, this documentary film explores how trees communicate with one another.

"Nalini Nadkarni: For the Love of Trees." YouTube video, 16:48. Posted by *National Geographic*, October 28, 2013. https://www.youtube.com/watch?v=7SwiRJJFm8Y. In this lecture, ecologist Nalini Nadkarni tells how scientists can better explain environmental problems to the nonscientific community.

"The Networked Beauty of Forests." YouTube video, 7:23. Posted by TED-Ed, April 14, 2014. https://www.youtube.com/watch?v=dRSPy3ZwpBk. Suzanne Simard discusses the Wood Wide Web in this TED Talk video.

"The Wood Wide Web." *Public Broadcasting Service*, February 2, 2017. http://www.pbs.org/wgbh/nova/nature/wood-wide-web.html. This short film examines the symbiotic relationship between tree roots and mycorrhizal fungi.

INDEX